# The
# Beginning

D0993913

LONDON, NEW YORK, MUNICH,
MELBOURNE, and DELHI

**Senior editor** David John
**Senior art editor** Joanne Connor
**Project art editor** Philip Letsu
**Managing editor** Andrew Macintyre
**Managing art editor** Jane Thomas
**Category publisher** Linda Martin
**Art director** Simon Webb
**Production controller** Erica Rosen
**DTP designer** Siu Yin Ho
**Picture researcher** Jo de Gray
**Picture librarians** Sarah Mills, Carl Strange
**Jacket Designer** Neal Cobourne

## Consultant
# David Lambert, MA

First published in Great Britain in 2003 by
Dorling Kindersley Limited
80 Strand, London WC2R 0RL

A Penguin Company

2 4 6 8 10 9 7 5 3 1

Copyright © 2003, 2004 Dorling Kindersley Limited
Text copyright © 2003 Peter Ackroyd

A CIP catalogue record for this book is
available from the British Library.

ISBN 1-4053-0692-0

Reproduced in Italy by G.R.B. Editrice, Verona
Printed and bound in China by L. Rex Printing Comany

See our complete catalogue at
www.dk.com

# Contents

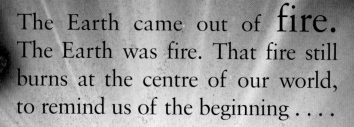

# The Earth came out of fire. The Earth was fire. That fire still burns at the centre of our world, to remind us of the beginning . . . .

In some unimaginable space that was no space, and time that was no time, there was once a great explosion of being out of nothingness called the Big Bang. Some 14 billion years ago, our Universe was born in a tiny speck, which was smaller than a pinhead and almost infinitely hot and dense. Within a few trillionths of a second, it exploded with such violence that matter started to form spontaneously out of energy. This matter became the future building material of planets and moons, stars and galaxies – everything we see in the night sky from the vantage of our tiny planet.

The infant Universe inflated at an unimaginable speed, as if it were already celebrating the birth of life and energy themselves. For three minutes, its raw energy produced a searing hot soup of subatomic particles. When those minutes had passed, the first savage heat was dispelled, and there followed 300,000 years before the temperature dropped low enough for the particles to form stable atoms of hydrogen and helium. As the fog of particles cleared, space became transparent. Over the next 300 million years, the hydrogen and the helium concentrated into dense clouds, with huge voids of space between them. Our Universe had by now entered a dark age from which it did not emerge for nearly a billion years. The gas clouds swirled through the dark aeons of time in a great cosmic dance until, slowly, they began to contract under the force of gravity and ignite to form galaxies filled with bright stars and glowing nebulas. Darkness gave birth to light.

When stars reach the end of their lives, some explode as supernovas.
Within these blasts are created carbon and nitrogen, iron and oxygen –
in fact, all the elements we know – which are then hurled out into
space. The human race itself is composed of materials that were forged
by supernovas. We carry within ourselves the traces of ancient stars.

So the galaxies revolved through time
and space, and one among their infinite
number is our own galaxy, the Milky Way.
It has four spiral arms, and today cradles
perhaps more than 200 billion stars. About
five billion years ago, in the Milky Way's Orion
arm, a vast cloud of gas and dust collapsed in
upon itself under the pressure of gravity. Conditions
at its centre became so hot and dense that nuclear fusion
took place and a new star was born in a blaze of radiation.

This was the star that became our Sun. As it condensed, it spun so fast
that it threw out a disc of gas and dust particles. As these particles
collided and stuck together, they formed dense spherical objects. Some
became rocky and hot, others large and gassy. These objects became the
nine planets of our Solar System, which still loop around the Sun in
regular or irregular orbits. It must already be clear that this is a
history of spheres and ellipses, of spirals and rotations.
The Universe loathes straight lines.

And so our Earth was formed.
More than 4,600 million years ago,
this fiery sphere, which we now
call home, rushed through space

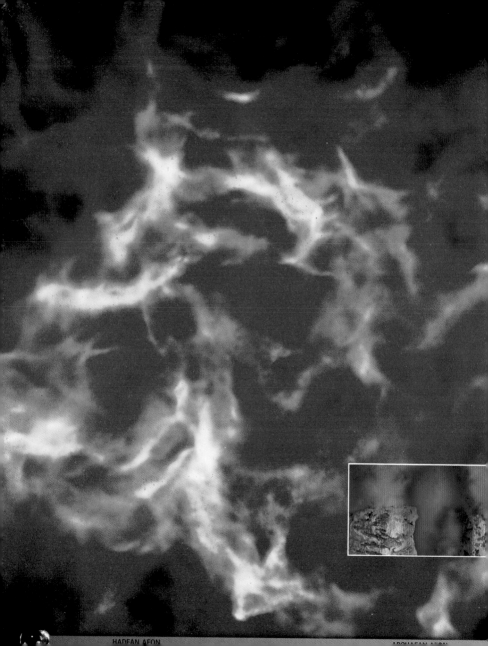

# CHAPTER ONE

# New heavens
## *and a new* earth

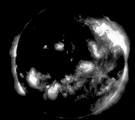

*So the world was born in the fire of galactic creation. The first age of the world is known as the* **Hadean** *– from Hades, the ancient Greek word for hell.*

THE EARTH, THEN, WAS LIKE HELL – a molten ball that reached a temperature of 5,000°C (9,000°F), fuelled by internal fire and by the impact of millions of meteorites raining down upon the revolving surface. The Earth blazed for 100 million years, until, slowly, the heavier metals of iron and nickel sank to the centre. There they formed a searing hot core that was more than 3,000 km (2,000 miles) in diameter. The lighter minerals rose to the surface, where after 100 million years they formed an outer layer almost 3,000 km (2,000 miles) thick. This makes up what we call the mantle of the Earth. These features have endured for more than 4,000 million years.

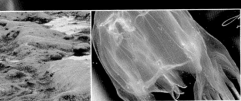

PROTEROZOIC AEON

TODAY

545 MILLION YEARS AGO

CAMBRIAN PERIOD
ORDOVICIAN PERIOD
SILURIAN PERIOD
DEVONIAN PERIOD
CARBONIFEROUS PERIOD
PERMIAN PERIOD
TRIASSIC PERIOD
JURASSIC PERIOD
CRETACEOUS PERIOD
TERTIARY PERIOD
QUATERNARY PERIOD

If we were to slice the Earth in two and peer into its interior, we would see a radioactive inner core of solid iron and nickel surrounded by a molten outer core. Above that lies the mantle, and on the mantle lies the crust. We live upon the Earth's crust, with a great fire far below us.

In the early Hadean world, in the rule of the inferno, there were chaos and destruction as well as fire. The new Earth had barely formed when it was struck by a fast-travelling object, about the size of Mars. The collision gouged out a great swathe of molten crust that splashed into space. After a billion years caught in orbit around the Earth, the ejected material eventually scrunched together under the pull of gravity. In this way, our Moon was born. The great cataclysm that created the Moon acts as a warning. It reminds us that the Earth is not independent of the Universe that surrounds it. Later we will come across other examples of how extraterrestrial forces violently changed the course of the Earth's history.

As the surface of the Earth cooled, solid areas of crust started to appear, rather like the skin that forms on congealing custard. The denser areas became ocean floor – the oceanic crust; the lighter crust formed into areas of land – the continental crust. Exactly when the crust formed

## Birth of the Moon

In our orbit around the Sun, we are accompanied by the Moon, the Earth's only natural satellite. Our Moon is unusual because it is very large in proportion to its planet. This is because it was born in a unique way. Most other moons are made from the debris left over after their planets formed. One or two were simply passing rocks captured by a planet's gravity. But our Moon formed after a massive object smashed into the Earth, splashing material out into orbit. We know this because the Moon contains pieces of our own planet as well as this other object.

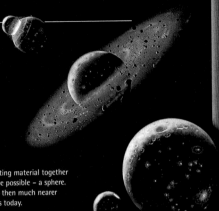

The young Earth takes a direct hit from a large rocky object hurtling through space.

The impact causes the Earth to re-melt. Huge amounts of crust and mantle are knocked into space.

Gravity pulls the orbiting material together into the densest shape possible – a sphere. The infant Moon was then much nearer to the Earth than it is today.

is still a mystery, the evidence having long been melted or eroded away. However, scientists have discovered some extremely ancient crystals of a mineral called zircon, which prove that there existed solid rocks at least as early as 4,400 million years ago.

The earliest atmosphere consisted of carbon dioxide, nitrogen, hydrogen and steam, which issued from cracks and vents in the Earth's mantle. This is known as "outgassing", a process that we can still see when volcanoes erupt. The steam, together with frozen water brought by comets that hit the Earth's surface, helped to create the first oceans.

The surface of the Earth had also begun to move. It is moving still. In the early days of the Earth's history, currents of heat, welling up from the core, together with intensive meteorite bombardments, caused the crust to crack into separate, moving sections called tectonic plates. These float like great ice floes on the Earth's semi-molten mantle. Today, there are about eight major tectonic plates, which tear apart, crash together or slide beneath each other at a rate of about 3 cm (1 in) each year. In doing so, they endlessly sculpt and mould the Earth's features. When two continental plates crush against each other, the crust buckles to form mountain ranges. The process takes millions upon millions of years. It is very hard to imagine mountains forming at such a slow rate, but this unthinkably long process reminds us of the immense age of the Earth. We have the illusion of living in a fixed world, but the ground beneath our feet is far from steady. Volcanoes and earthquakes are violent reminders that the tectonic plates never stop moving.

During the Earth's infancy, volcanic activity made conditions on the surface unimaginably turbulent and hostile. Yet somehow, in this desolation of lava and ash, this world lashed by meteorites and acid rain, life spontaneously erupted. How this miracle happened is still the subject of much theory and debate. It was once thought that life began with the spark of a

Core is kept solid by pressure.

Molten outer core

Semi-molten mantle

Rocks circulate in mantle.

Solid crust

**WARM HEART**
The Earth is made of three main layers – the thin surface crust, the mantle and the very hot core. Heat from the core causes the semi-molten rocks in the mantle to circulate slowly. This flow, known as convection, disturbs the surface crust, making it move in vast slabs called tectonic plates.

Tectonic plates grind past each other at the San Andreas fault in California, USA.

sudden lightning strike. In a famous experiment of the 1950s, an electrical discharge, passed through a mixture of ammonia, methane, steam and hydrogen – thought to be the equivalent of the Earth's atmosphere at the time – created certain complex substances. Amino acids were among them. These are chemicals that link together to form proteins, the building blocks of life.

But scientists now know that the early atmosphere was rich in carbon dioxide, and that such experiments do not produce amino acids from a carbon-dioxide atmosphere. One theory looks in a different direction for an answer. We know that the young Earth suffered intense bombardments of meteorites and asteroids. Could life have begun with certain molecules

A meteorite heats up as it enters the atmosphere.

**ORIGINS IN SPACE?**
In 1996, a meteorite from Mars was found to contain what looked like fossilized bacteria. It is possible that simple, bacterial life once evolved on Mars and other places in the Solar System.

## Moving plates

The Earth's tectonic plates move in three ways – they tear apart, collide, or grind past one another. Where two plates pull apart, molten rock from the mantle rises to fill the gap. If this happens on the ocean floor, it creates an underwater spreading ridge. Where two plates collide, they either ripple to form mountain ranges, or else one sinks below the other and melts in a process known as subduction. This may force lava to the surface, causing volcanoes to erupt. Where plates slide past each other, a transform fault appears and earthquakes may occur. Often a long fault line appears on the Earth's surface.

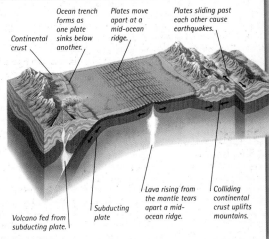

Ocean trench forms as one plate sinks below another.

Continental crust

Plates move apart at a mid-ocean ridge.

Plates sliding past each other cause earthquakes.

Lava rising from the mantle tears apart a mid-ocean ridge.

Colliding continental crust uplifts mountains.

Subducting plate

Volcano fed from subducting plate.

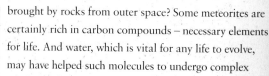

**EXTREME LIFE**
Life can flourish even in extreme conditions. These "heat-loving" bacteria live inside volcanic vents.

brought by rocks from outer space? Some meteorites are certainly rich in carbon compounds – necessary elements for life. And water, which is vital for any life to evolve, may have helped such molecules to undergo complex changes. But scientists are still not sure how molecules like these could have assembled themselves into the Earth's very first life forms.

So what were these first living organisms? What kind of life could have survived in the young world's infernal climate? The atmosphere of carbon dioxide would not have been suitable for any plant or animal life known to us now. The glimmerings of an answer may be found in the inky depths of the sea. Today, near volcanic hot vents upon the ocean floor known as black smokers, there live simple, single-celled microbes that can survive in extreme heat. These microbes, called thermophiles, positively thrive in boiling temperatures. They do not need sunlight or even oxygen. In just the same way, primitive life flourished in the hot volcanic soup disgorged through vents in the ancient ocean floors. The first life forms on the Earth were no more than these simple microbes – faint smears covering rocks, so delicate in the elemental fury all around. Yet here was original life itself.

This early life emerged during what is known as Pre-Cambrian time. It begins 4,560 million years ago, with the formation of the Earth, and ends 545 million years ago. These simple figures represent a length of time that is almost impossible to comprehend. It can only brood in the background of our minds – a vast immensity of time from which life emerged blinking into the light. Pre-Cambrian time covers seven-eighths of the world's history, most of which will remain unknown to us. It does not represent solely

**EARLY ALGAE**
In time, microbes helped to build complex cells like those that form this living colony of *Volvox*, a type of algae.

**BLACK SMOKERS**

Strange vents on the deep sea floor belch out clouds of volcanically heated, sulphur-rich water. Around them mounds of mineral deposits build up into chimney-like stacks. These are known as black smokers. Despite the extreme heat, and in conditions that mirror those of the early Earth, life thrives in these places.

**SUN FOOD**
Cyanobacteria such as these were the first life forms to use the Sun's energy to make food.

the birth or childhood of the world, as some suggest, but rather the birth, childhood, youth and middle age of the world. We are, in fact, living at the beginning of the world's old age.

We have found no fossil remains of the very first forms of life, because no rocks could have survived the continuous pounding and pulverizing of the emerging world. But scientists may have discovered the first clues in rocks dated at about 3,800 million years. These rocks, found in Greenland, contain traces of a type of carbon that could be the

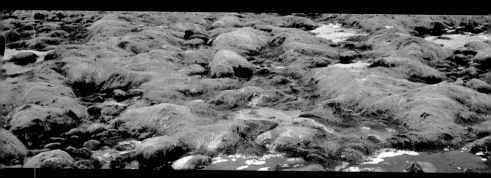

**SCUM SURVIVORS**
Algae have survived unchanged for millions of years. Their enduring success lies in an ability to withstand severe environmental stresses, such as drying out and bashing by waves.

fingerprint of life, because it is usually found in living organisms. The carbon is possibly what remains of the early microbes. If true, then its presence in such ancient rocks means that life began very early indeed – as soon as conditions on the new planet were stable enough to let it take hold. But the earliest actual fossil evidence of life may lie in certain rocks dating back 3,500 million years. These snake-like, microscopic fossils look like lines of beads packed tightly together. They may be the remains of cyanobacteria – primitive, single-celled algae that are related to the slimy stuff still found on the surface of slow or stagnant water. When you trail your finger in the green scum of a pond, you could be touching life that has remained unchanged for almost 3,500 million years.

The ancient cyanobacteria probably thrived near the sunlit surfaces of the seas, using the energy in sunlight to make food and protein. Over time, these tiny organisms helped to form colonies of mushroom-shaped mats, known as stromatolites, which grew from seabeds and solidified. Stromatolites survive even today in shallow seas as a reminder that the original, basic world is still with us. It is almost as if we can see, touch and study life's origins. The billions of single-celled organisms that made up the ancient stromatolites absorbed carbon dioxide and enriched the early atmosphere with oxygen. Over millions of years, the amount of oxygen in the atmosphere increased until there was enough to sustain all subsequent life forms. Emerging life was steadily creating the conditions for more life. It is worth remembering this astounding process when we are faced with the muddle and mayhem of our modern lives – in the deep structures of the world, everything connects.

**ATMOSPHERE BUILDERS**
The tiny organisms that make up these stromatolites do not require oxygen. They ingest carbon dioxide and release oxygen as waste.

**ORIGIN UNKNOWN**
Some early life is difficult to classify. This life form, extracted from a Silurian-period rock, is a single-celled organism known as an "acritarch", meaning "of uncertain origin".

Until about 2,000 million years ago, the only living forms on the Earth were simple microbes, such as the primitive cyanobacteria. Each one was no more than a single cell and reproduced by dividing in two. Over time, some types of microbes absorbed others, and became larger cells, each with a cell nucleus. Eventually, these combined and "specialized" to form tissues and organs in one many-celled body. This allowed increasingly complex life forms to flourish and evolve. The result was a dramatic evolutionary leap towards the

end of Pre-Cambrian time, when animals began to appear. The earliest possible traces of animal activity are fossilized burrows made by some kind of wormlike creature, dated at about 1,200 million years old.

The last division of Pre-Cambrian time is called the Vendian period. By this time, all manner of wonderful life forms had evolved from the original, primitive single cells. In the Ediacara Hills of southern Australia, the rocks are riddled with the fossils of an extraordinary range of Vendian life. About 600 million years after the first signs of animal activity, life itself seems to have exploded. This is one of the patterns of prehistory, a sudden blossoming of life after periods of slow activity or extinction, as if evolution occurs not by gradual development but in

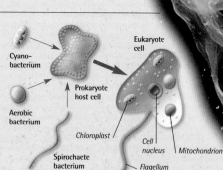

**SOFT IMPRESSIONS**
Amazingly, soft and delicate animals occasionally leave impressions in sediment that turns to rock. Some of the earliest complex fossils found resemble jellyfish, like this one.

## How complex life evolved

About 2,000 million years ago, large, complex cells called eukaryotes emerged. They had somehow evolved out of primitive, simple microbes called prokaryotes. But how? It seems that one type of prokaryote may have "swallowed" other types of prokaryote. Rather than digesting them, the host prokaryote protected its captives. Over time, the captive prokaryotes evolved to become important parts, called organelles, of the new eukaryote cell, carrying out functions such as respiration and photosynthesis. One prokaryote may even have become a basic "tail" to help the eukaryote move about.

Cyano-bacterium

Aerobic bacterium

Prokaryote host cell

Chloroplast

Spirochaete bacterium

Eukaryote cell

Cell nucleus

Mitochondrion

Flagellum

The prokaryote host cell captures and protects the bacteria. In the new cell that evolves, the cyanobacterium becomes a chloroplast, which uses the energy in sunlight to make food.

The aerobic bacterium becomes a mitochondrion, which uses oxygen as a source of energy. Most importantly, the new cell has evolved a nucleus, which contains genetic material.

sudden, amazing bursts. This may, of course, be simply the accident of discovery, when a rich layer of rock is uncovered by chance. If this is the case, then we must imagine a world in which life was always more diverse and plentiful than people think. The Earth may have been seething with life in earlier times, too.

In the Ediacara Hills there are fossilized jellyfish, and worms, and strange feather-like creatures known as sea-pens. Some of these creatures would have remained motionless on the seabed, while others would have drifted. Some had two sides, others were blobs or globules of transparent matter. There were other organisms that seemed to be in the process of developing a primitive head. Yet what kind of creatures were they? Certain types had a bizarre, quilted texture and appear unrelated to any living species. These were experiments in life that failed. It is wonderful to think of primitive life that was truly alien once living in the same seas as our distant ancestors. There are even some scientists who believe that all the fossils found in the Ediacara Hills are snapshots of a "wrong turn" in the life forms of the Earth, and that they only look like modern creatures by accident. They represent a dead end in evolutionary history.

We have enough evidence to suppose, however, that in this mysterious Pre-Cambrian time, there were some complex, multi-celled life forms that somehow managed to cross the abyss known as an extinction event, and survive into the next period, the Cambrian.

**STONE PATTERN**
The fossil *Mawsonites* is one of the earliest multi-celled organisms. Similar to a jellyfish, it lived at the end of the Pre-Cambrian, some 550 million years ago.

**SEA-PEN RELATIONS**
Modern sea-pens such as these resemble Pre-Cambrian types called *Charnia*. Scientists still dispute whether the two are related.

# CHAPTER TWO

# Life *takes* hold

*A giant transition marked the beginning of the **Cambrian** period, about 545 million years ago. In much of the world, the old marine life disappeared.*

WE STILL DO NOT FULLY UNDERSTAND the reason for this great extinction. It is possible that the defenceless, soft-bodied creatures we have described were hunted to oblivion by newly evolved predators. The arrival of sea creatures with defensive shells and armour plating certainly suggests that the oceans had become more dangerous for animals without protection. This, coupled with the endless movement of the tectonic plates, which may have caused shallow-sea habitats to dry out and disappear, was probably enough to extinguish many of the bizarre life forms of the Pre-Cambrian. We have already seen how the tectonic plates move, now drifting apart and now crashing into each other, and as a result, the geography of the world long ago would

PROTEROZOIC AEON

CAMBRIAN PERIOD | 545–495 MILLION YEARS AGO TODAY

have been completely unrecognizable to us. Towards the end of Pre-Cambrian time, two vast landmasses dominated the globe. These have been named Northern Gondwana and Southern Gondwana. The northern landmass contained areas that are now called India, Australia and Antarctica; the southern landmass contained Africa, North and South America, and a large part of Asia. The world was upside down. Africa and South America were tethered somewhere near the South Pole and, at the end of the Pre-Cambrian, were covered in sheets of ice. When you look at any map of the Earth in this remote time it looks bewildering, both familiar and unfamiliar, the product of great forces that still shape the world today. About 580 million years ago, Northern Gondwana and Southern Gondwana slowly collided and formed an even greater landmass. Indeed, it was the only landmass on the Earth, and has been named Pannotia. This new continent was short-lived, lasting for only a few tens of millions of years, and by the beginning of the Cambrian period was breaking up into smaller continents.

The Cambrian period began 545 million years ago and lasted for some 50 million years. In this topsy-turvy phase of the

**RIDDLE OF THE SHELLS**
By examining the shapes of these ancient creatures' shells, scientists speculate that *Tommotia* may have been a squid-like animal with grasping tentacles, *Hyolithellus* a slender-tentacled mollusc, and *Latouchella* a snail-like form with a creeping foot.

Tommotia

Hyolithellus

Earth's history, Greenland enjoyed a semi-tropical climate, and China still lay beneath the ocean. North America was part of a continent named Laurentia, and was joined with Scotland and Greenland. England and Wales were beneath the sea, where they were connected with what are now Newfoundland, Canada, and New England, USA. This sunken continental fragment has been named Avalonia in homage to the island of Avalon in Celtic myth. It is intriguing how various legends, including that of the lost continent of Atlantis, seem to have some foundation in the events of prehistory.

The Cambrian world was one of origination, when millions of new species emerged with energy and diversity in what is known as "the Cambrian explosion". The fossils from this time reveal the abundance and variety of marine life, some of which can be recognized and classified, but some will remain mysterious and inexplicable. New life forms were filling the void left by the extinction of the old. There was an early Cambrian creature, named *Halkieria*, which had a sausage-shaped body, covered in scaly plates, and a shell-like cap at either end. There were creatures otherwise unknown except for the tiny protective spines they left behind. The seas teemed with fantastic life forms.

**HALKIERIA'S COAT**
Scientists originally thought that Cambrian fossil shells like this one housed tiny limpet-like creatures. In fact, the shells may not have belonged to separate creatures at all but to a scaly, plated coat that covered the slug-like animal *Halkieria*.

Latouchella

What is striking about the Cambrian period, however, in relation to the previous 3,000 million years of the Earth's history, is the arrival of creatures with shells. They emerge all over the world at about the same time, as if answering to some great instinct or need. Creatures named *Hyolithellus* and *Tommotia* lived inside hollow, horn-like shells resembling

pointed hats. Indeed, only the shells have been found so we must guess at the nature of whatever tentacled or slug-like animals lived inside them. They may have been ancestors of the cephalopods – the group that today includes octopuses and squids.

Some scientists suggest that shells evolved as a means of storing or filtering nutrients, but the main theory argues that shells were basically a form of self-defence – a way of warding off predators. This signals an important change in the condition of life on the Earth. Struggle for survival has now entered the equation. It is in some ways a sad discovery, since it suggests that the instinct for aggression and competition has a very long history indeed.

**TEEMING TRILOBITES**
Before fishes became dominant, the seas teemed with trilobites, relatives of today's woodlice, crabs and insects. Most trilobites crawled, but some swam.

The oxygen in the atmosphere was now growing more plentiful, but life itself was still confined to the oceans of the world. Living upon the seabed were molluscs and worms and various forms of crustacean. About one-third of all fossils discovered from the Cambrian period are those of a strange type of creature known as a trilobite. It looked a little like a woodlouse, with a hard protective covering. Its shell had three lobes, or sections. Trilobites could crawl over the seafloor on their many-jointed legs and, like woodlice, could roll themselves into a protective ball if threatened. They have survived as fossils in immense numbers – there are remains of more than 15,000 species of this creature, ranging in size from ones that can only be seen under a

## The eye of a trilobite

The eyes found in trilobites were among the earliest eyes to evolve. There were two main types of eye, each made up of tiny calcite-crystal lenses. Most trilobites had holochroal eyes, which resembled the compound eyes of today's insects. Up to 15,000 six-sided lenses were closely packed like cells in a honeycomb. Each lens pointed in a slightly different direction. Holochroal eyes formed fuzzy images of anything that moved. Other trilobites had schizochroal eyes, which contained large, ball-shaped lenses. Schizochroal eyes produced sharp images of objects.

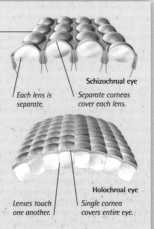

Schizochroal eye

Each lens is separate.

Separate corneas cover each lens.

Holochroal eye

Lenses touch one another.

Single cornea covers entire eye.

microscope to others that were 30 cm (12 in) long. One was even found in a French cave, known as Grotte du Trilobite, where some Stone-Age humans had preserved it as a magic charm or totem. The sheer range of trilobites, all now extinct, testifies to the diversity of prehistoric life. But the most extraordinary features of the trilobite were its eyes. Trilobites were among the earliest creatures on the Earth that could see well. And their eyes were not simple organs at all. Some were made up of many thousands of lenses, each having six sides, which were packed closely together under the protection of a cornea (the transparent cover of the lens). Each lens was made of calcite crystal, a substance similar to the mineral known as Iceland spar, which refracted light. Thousands of these lenses would then create a mosaic portrait of the world. This trilobite's-eye view was the first clear picture of the world since its creation. Even in these early stages of its existence, life was already enormously complicated.

Scientists have found another astonishing portrait of the Cambrian world in the Rocky Mountains of British Columbia, Canada. There, in the mudstone known as the Burgess Shale, a spectacular range of ancient sea creatures has been uncovered. Among the fossils found are trilobites as well as sponges, jellyfish and worm-like organisms. Some of the "worms" have spikes; others have teeth. There was one curious animal, named *Hallucigenia* because of its dream-like appearance.

**CAMBRIAN KING**
*Anomalocaris* ("odd shrimp") was an elegant, slow-moving predator. The creature's powerful, prawn-like arms would have grasped and twisted prey inwards towards its mouth.

**DREAM WALKING**
Scientists once thought *Hallucigenia* walked on spiny stilts, while waving its soft tentacles upwards in search of food. Later findings literally turned this interpretation upside down. The spines pointed upwards for protection.

No one is sure which end
was its head and which its tail. It
typifies the sheer strangeness of the
Cambrian world. Another animal, named
*Opabinia*, was a predatory "worm" with five
eyes and a long, flexible nozzle that ended in a
set of spiny jaws. Scientists have declared it an
unclassifiable puzzle. There was also a giant among
sea animals. *Anomalocaris* was some 60 cm (24 in) long,
and seemed to be part jellyfish, part shrimp and part sea cucumber.
The diversity of life encouraged all these strange forms, as if life as
we now know it emerged from a phantasmagoria, a fantasy-like
mixture of shape and size.

It is natural for us to imagine the sea life of the Cambrian period being
as grey as the fossil forms that have survived, but there is no reason to
doubt that there was plenty of colour and shading. On the ocean beds
of today's world there are creatures that shimmer with strange lights,
or whose lights whirl or pulsate with the currents of the ocean. The
Cambrian seas were no doubt glimmering with ancient lights, like
some primeval rock concert. Except, of course, that there was no

sound: apart from the howling wind and the breaking of the seas on the shores of the world there was a universal silence. It was a world without calls or cries, without song or scream. For millions of years there was just the noise of the elements and the endless churning of the waves.

There was one other fossil in the Burgess Shale that is of enormous importance in the story of the Earth. It came from a sea animal known as *Pikaia*, a worm-like creature about 5 cm (2 in) long. It might seem very ordinary at first glance, until we learn that creatures such as this gave rise to those with backbones made of vertebrae. *Pikaia* was a chordate, or an animal with a notochord (a rod for stiffening the body), and as such was probably related to the ancestor of all the vertebrates of the Earth – fishes, amphibians, reptiles, birds and of course mammals, which include us. Creatures such as the tiny *Pikaia* really were the mother and father of humankind.

It is interesting to see how the earliest vertebrates, including jawless fishes, had evolved heads. In their continual search for food, fish-like chordates had to be able to smell, touch and even see the surrounding areas of water. Somehow, this combined search for information led to the development of a nerve cord with a front-end swelling that eventually became a brain. You can see how the shape we are today is directly related to the need to adapt and to control what immediately surrounds us.

**PRE-VERTEBRATE**
The sea animal *Pikaia* swam in a wave-like motion by contracting the muscles along its notochord. *Pikaia* gave rise to animals with vertebrae.

HADEAN AEON                                    ARCHAEAN AEON

# CHAPTER THREE

# The invasion *of* land

*Many creatures of the Cambrian survived into the next long period of the Earth's history, the* **Ordovician.** *This is dated from 494 to 443 million years ago.*

THIS PERIOD OF 50 MILLION YEARS began only after another vast extinction of life. There were in fact two mass extinctions in the Cambrian period – not sudden events but rather slow catastrophes that unfolded over millions of years. They were caused by the Earth's shifting tectonic plates. As continents collided, the shallow sea habitats of many marine species were squeezed out of existence. Scientists estimate that in one extinction event, more than 70 per cent of those species were destroyed. It is as if new life can only spring out of the destruction of the old.

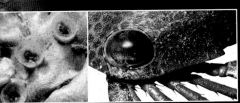

At the beginning of the Ordovician, Australia was covered in shallow seas, and North Africa was over what is now the South Pole. North America and northern Europe were slowly moving together. The western edges of the British Isles were dominated by a ring of volcanic islands. Throughout this period there were great climatic changes, some of them the result of volcanic eruptions. And, as we shall see, the Ordovician came to an end in the grip of a long ice age. The Earth seems always to hover between fire and ice.

**TINY TEETH**
Conodonts were tiny sea animals that survived for about 300 million years before dying out. These fossilized conodont teeth are shown on a pinhead.

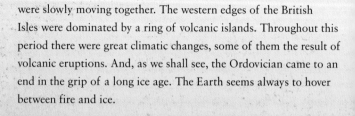

But this was also a period in which early vertebrate life, which first appeared with creatures similar to the tiny *Pikaia*, survived and prospered. Jawless fishes grew bony body armour. Small, eel-like creatures called conodonts had large eyes, teeth, muscles like a fish's, even fins, but they were jawless, too. Evidence suggests that they swam in shoals through the Ordovician seas. But, ultimately, they were swimming into oblivion. They are now only part of the fossil record and have left no living survivors. In the gradual evolution of the fishes, conodonts were another experiment that failed.

There was, however, an abundance of other sea life in an age that was dominated by the oceans. The invertebrates (animals without a backbone) were also flourishing. There were corals and sea snails, sponges and brachiopods, trilobites and all manner of other creatures with shells. There were sea lilies and burrowing clams, starfishes and sea urchins. Some of these groups had evolved as "filter feeders", living off the teeming plankton in the water. The web of life was by now organized in a complex way – a vast system of interconnected food chains linked eaters with eaten from plankton upwards. In appearance, many of the invertebrates

**PRICKLY CREATURES**
Sea urchins first appeared during the Ordovician. These invertebrates evolved a spiny armour as defence against predators.

**STARS OF THE SEA**
Starfishes have remained almost unchanged since primeval times. They have five sucker-tipped feet, no head and no brain.

**MARINE ODDITY**
*Cothurnocystis* may have dragged itself along the seabed by its tail. Scientists are not sure if it was an ancestor of fishes or if it belonged to the same group as sea urchins.

resembled the inhabitants of today's oceans, which suggests that some aspects of Earth life have not changed very much at all. The main difference lies in the fact that invertebrates were the predominant forms of life. Their fossils make delicate shapes in the ancient stone as if they were the inhabitants of some light and buoyant kingdom.

Especially delicate are the fossils of what are called graptolites, or written stones, because their remains look like shining lines of handwriting. Graptolites were organized colonies of little cups, linked together along a strand. From each cup there poked a tiny, frilly-headed, filter-feeding animal known as a zooid. Their colonies were plentiful in the oceans of the Ordovician. Some were tethered to the seafloor while others floated at the surface, drifting downwards when

**UNDERWATER GARDENS**
Many ancient varieties of coral thrived in the warm shallows of the Ordovician seas, forming extensive reefs.

they died, until they lay upon the sediment in which they were eventually fossilized. Millions of years passed as these fragile creatures were turned into stone.

There were larger and fiercer creatures, too. Cephalopod ("head-footed") molluscs, known as straight-shelled nautiloids, grew to 4 m (12.5 ft) in length. Nothing on the Earth had ever grown so large. The largest were true monsters of the deep.

**JET PROPULSION**
Giant nautiloids could dart after prey at speed by squirting a jet of water backwards from their body cavity. They could even rise or dive like submarines by adjusting the level of gas inside their shells.

But, for all the dramatic evolution taking place in the oceans, there was a transition of much greater importance in the Ordovician period. Life began its invasion of the land. First there came the plants or, rather, their ancestors the green algae, which moved from the sea into freshwater areas. Then liverworts – low-growing plants with dark green, ribbon-like leaves – began to creep across the ground, and for the first time in the world's history life began to survive on land. There was now enough oxygen for respiration and a strong enough layer of sun-shielding ozone gas in the high atmosphere to protect these primitive plants, which grew along the edges of water

**BUDDING LIFE**
Liverworts are among the most ancient of plants. Some varieties reproduce by creating these tiny buds (gemmae) on their leaves. The buds develop into new plants.

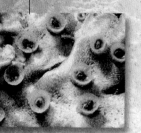

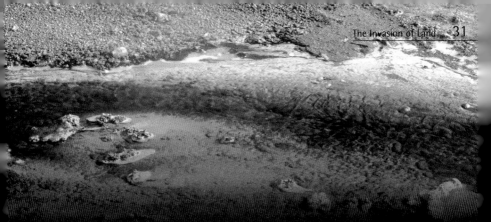

nd in dim, damp caves. The plants were followed by tiny tracks. Geologists in Canada have discovered the oldest footprints in the history of the world. They were made by the jointed legs of a small arthropod – a creature, therefore, that belonged to the same great group of invertebrates that today includes insects, spiders, scorpions and crustaceans. This particular creature was much like a woodlouse. t crawled out of the fresh water and took the first steps of any creature on dry land. Its track is only a centimetre wide, but it heralds the great movement of creatures from the sea onto the land. t is strange to see these tiny markings, the first faint signals of a giant transition. The first living things had come up into the air. The earliest plants spread under the Sun, and the first creatures began their slow track across the Earth. Life seems instinctively to spread outwards and to colonize new territories.

Some life forms of the Ordovician period still exist. The little mussel-like brachiopod known as *Lingula*, for example, has remained about the same. But many did not survive. This long period in the Earth's history was terminated by a giant ice age. Africa became a sheet of ce. The cold was so intense, and the glaciation so widespread, that

**CARPETS OF GREEN**
Green algae were the first life forms to survive on land. The oxygen they released continued to build the Earth's atmosphere.

**FIRST STEPS**
Small crustaceans, somewhat like these woodlice, were the first animals to move from water to land.

half of the world's species disappeared. It was a wholesale extermination. Yet out of it emerged new forms of life. About 443 million years ago, the Earth entered the Silurian period.

The oceans now grew warmer and their level rose as the great sheets of ice melted. Indeed, one ocean covered almost half the globe. This was the mighty Panthalassic Ocean. Those species that survived the long ice age had adapted to the changed conditions. The seas teemed once again with fishes.

Jawless fishes were still plentiful, but now, jawed fishes began to come into their own. One group were the placoderms, a name meaning "plated skin". These shark-like vertebrates grew only to 60 cm (24 in) in length at first, and were encased in cumbersome plates so that they looked like small armoured vehicles. Placoderms were highly successful in their habitat, but by the end of the next period, the Devonian, they, too, had entered the endless night of extinction. In their evolutionary lifetime of about 70 million years they swam among sea lilies, which, despite their name, are in fact animals with long stems anchored to the seabed. The Silurian seas were filled with these little creatures, thriving in such abundance and diversity that the Earth might have been

**"ARMS" AND ARMOUR**
This placoderm had jointed, bony "arms" for punting along the seabed. Its plated body armour has been preserved in this fossil.

**TENTACLE TRAP**
The tentacles of this fossil sea lily were used to gather floating food.

known as the planet of the sea lily. Vast coral reefs, too, were formed in the Silurian period, among which there lurked ferocious, predatory sea scorpions, 2 m (7ft) in length, complete with massive claws. If you can imagine a lobster longer than a man, then you have some idea of this nightmarish Silurian creature.

**SCORPION CLAWS**
*Pterygotus* was the largest species of Silurian sea scorpion. It would lie in ambush before seizing and tearing its prey apart with pincer-like fangs.

Evolution surged marvellously forwards once the journey from the sea to the land had begun. The first small steps of the Ordovician had by now become a confident progress. We can classify the Silurian as that period when living organisms first truly invaded the land and made it their home.

**ANCIENT ARTHROPODS**
Centipedes are among the most ancient of today's creatures. These many-legged scavengers and predators evolved from aquatic ancestors more than 410 million years ago.

First came the reign of the plants, followed by the arrival of invertebrate animals. The first land plants had been the liverworts, with their leaves lying flat upon the ground like the scales of a fish. Liverworts and lichens had arrived in Ordovician times and all were creeping forms. Now, by some innovative explosion of plant life, there appeared along the edges of ponds and streams plants that grew upright. They reached towards the Sun. By developing supporting fibres and inner tubes that acted as channels for moisture, they were able to remain vertical. These are known as vascular plants – from the Latin word *vasculum*, meaning a small container – and among them were the ancestors of every kind of land plant now alive. With a new ability to retain moisture, plants could travel further from the edges of water. In this way, they could begin to colonize the land. The first upright plant has been named *Cooksonia*. It grew to a height of about 10 cm (4 in) and had neither leaves nor roots, but rather a simple structure with branching stems. On the tips of the stems were little caps holding spores (reproductive cells) that were carried aloft on the prehistoric wind. There were other plants that crept upwards, among them a relative of today's clubmoss that grew stems of 25 cm (10 in). These had tiny, feathery

leaves covering them like fur. From early, leafless vascular plants would in time come all the leafy plants of today. The surface of the Earth was still largely one of desert and barren stone, a wilderness of rock, but now a green smudge or blur was beginning to spread outwards from the banks of rivers and streams, like the breath of life itself. These early plants were also issuing more oxygen into the atmosphere, so enabling other living organisms to grow and flourish in this inhospitable landscape.

Creatures had begun to colonize the land, too. Geologists have uncovered the marks and scratches of tiny Silurian creatures in the sandstones of Western Australia. These arthropods included millipedes, scorpions and trigonotarbids, which were early relatives of the spiders. If you look at such creatures today, they seem self-sufficient, empowered by some dark source of energy. Many people are frightened of scorpions and spiders because they scuttle quickly and can be dangerous; they are watchful and predatory. But perhaps people also sense that such creatures come out of some unknown prehistoric past. The arthropods of the Silurian ate other arthropods, or lived upon mites, which in turn fed off rotting vegetation. The food chain was now established on land.

**NEW PLANTS**
The stems on this moss plant each hold a capsule containing thousands of spores. When released, they will germinate into miniature new plants. Spores enabled the earliest plants, such as *Cooksonia*, to occupy land.

# CHAPTER FOUR

# The age *of* fishes

*About 417 million years ago, as the* **Devonian** *period began, great changes took place on the Earth. North America and Europe were colliding, creating huge mountains.*

THE APPALACHIAN MOUNTAINS in the eastern United States, the Scottish Highlands and the mountains of Scandinavia – now all distant from each other – are the remains of a single, enormous mountain chain that formed at this time in the Earth's history. Colliding lands also formed mountains in Australia. These great Earth movements are the monumental backdrop to what is known as the Devonian period, which lasted more than 60 million years, stretching from 417 million years ago to 354 million years ago. It was the period that witnessed the emergence of vertebrate life upon the land. It has also been called "the age of fishes".

Although some parts of the Earth's surface were extremely dry, bare of vegetation and dusted by hot winds,

**ARMOURED SNOUT**
The small jawless fish
*Pteraspis* may have swum
near the surface of the
Devonian seas, guzzling
shrimp-like creatures. Its
heavily armoured head had
a peculiar pointed snout.

much of the world was still under water. The
level of the oceans was very high, and the two
supercontinents of Gondwana and Laurentia were
crisscrossed with rivers and streams and dotted with
inland seas and lakes where freshwater life flourished.
The seas themselves teemed with countless life forms. There
were bony fishes, fishes with jaws and fishes without jaws, fishes with
fleshy fins and fishes with spiny fins, fishes like tadpoles and fishes like
eels and molluscs of a thousand different groups. One group of
molluscs, the ammonoids, first appeared in this period. Their large flat
shells, curled like rams' horns, can be bought in every fossil shop. Inside
each of them there originally lived a tentacled creature with beak-like
jaws that combed the seabed for food.

Ammonoids are but one type of fossil among many. Throughout the
long and slow history of the world, plants and animals have died and
their bodies have been covered by sediment such as sand or mud.
Usually, the buried plants and animals rot away completely, but now
and then an organism's fragile remains are gradually replaced by
minerals. Over untold millions of years, the surrounding sediment is
slowly turned into rock, and a fossil is formed. But the fossil record
of early life is very incomplete. There were many more living species
than there are fossils; many soft-bodied creatures will have wholly
disappeared from the Earth. Only a fraction of existing fossils has been
found. There may be whole groups of creatures that have not yet been
identified, although new finds are being made all the time. Who knows
what strange creature will emerge from the rocks of unexplored regions,
overturning some widely held theory about life in the prehistoric past?

**FOSSIL DATING**
Ammonoids have left a
rich fossil record. Known
species from particular
periods are useful for
dating rocks.

With the arrival of larger vertebrate predators, the Devonian seas
became the arena for an intense struggle for survival. Most fishes
fled from the larger placoderms, which had become the greatest

vertebrate hunters of the time. These armour-plated fishes had first emerged in the Silurian period, but now many were faster, more powerful and more ferocious. A formidable placoderm, named *Dunkleosteus* ("Dunkle's Bony One") after the scientist who discovered it, grew to a length of 5 m (16 ft). It had a jointed neck and could seize its prey with the razor-sharp, plate-like teeth in its jaws. Other placoderms grew as long as 8 m (26 ft), and were easily the largest vertebrates yet to inhabit the seas. Some species of

**BONY ONE**
*Dunkleosteus* had a colossal head and jaws, fitted with razor-like teeth that became sharper as the creature bit and ate.

placoderm, such as *Gemuendina*, were flat-bodied, ray-like forms with sharp teeth. Others had begun to grow primitive "arms" with which to forage for food on the seabed. Most of them had long "tails" like those of rats.

In these dangerous seas swam early sharks. They bore a remarkable resemblance to the menacing creatures that continue to stalk the oceans more than 400 million years later, and so provide an outstanding example of an evolutionary formula that has stood the test of time. Their vicious, primitive power no doubt accounts for the fear and fascination that they have always instilled in people. Early species had a different kind of snout and mouth from those living today, but their tails and fins, their pointed teeth, their streamlined bodies and their skeletons made not of bone but of a firm, flexible substance called cartilage show that they were genuine sharks.

There were also "spiny sharks", a completely different group of fishes, with fins like pointed teeth. These mostly small animals were incredibly successful and survived for some 170 million years, about a thousand times longer than *Homo sapiens* has lived upon the Earth. It is most

**FOSSIL RAY**
*Gemuendina* swam with rippling movements of its side fins. It thrust out its jaws to crush shellfish.

**SPINY SHARKS**
The ancient spiny sharks had large eyes. Unlike modern sharks, they hunted by sight, not scent.

unlikely that humans will last so long. Like most other Devonian fishes, the spiny sharks evolved and survived in the sea, but then made the transition to freshwater lakes and rivers. They were one of the four groups of jawed fishes that between them eventually killed off or out-competed the vast majority of jawless fishes. On a local level it was just a matter of one fish tracking down another, but over millions of years this resulted in the extinctions of entire species.

Perhaps the most extraordinary survivor from the Devonian, however, is a type of large bony fish known as a coelacanth. Scientists had long believed that such tassel-tailed creatures had died out more than 50 million years ago, so we may imagine their surprise when one was caught off the South African coast in 1938. Other individuals have since been found. With its wide mouth and enamelled scales, a coelacanth does indeed look like some creature dredged from the depths of time – truly a living fossil. Coelacanths and lungfishes are the only survivors of a once great group known as the

**DESIGN SUCCESS**
The basic features
of today's sharks –
dagger-like fangs and a
torpedo-shaped body –
have remained the same
since Devonian times.

**A LIVING FOSSIL**
The coelacanth's fleshy
lobes and tassel tail have
remained unchanged in
350 million years.

## From fins to legs

The first four-legged animals (tetrapods) evolved from lobe-finned fishes during the Devonian. Bones supporting these fishes' fins developed into limbs with wrist and elbow joints, probably as a means of propulsion in shallow waters. These animals illustrate the stages in this evolutionary process.

**Eusthenopteron**
Two front and rear fins of this fish contained bone structures similar to those found in the limbs of the first tetrapods.

**Panderichthys**
This fish's features were closer to those of an early tetrapod than a fish. It had a long flat head and fins resembling primitive limbs.

**Acanthostega**
This predator had a tail fin and gills like a fish's, but also eight-digit hands used to move among water plants.

**Temnospondyls**
This group of tetrapods had developed limbs, ribs and a backbone robust enough to support their weight on land.

lobe-finned fishes, which flourished in Devonian times. Unlike ray-finned bony fishes (most kinds alive today), lobe-fins, as the name suggests, sprouted fins from muscular "lobes", or projections, on the body. In fact, some of them developed fins that were sturdy enough to resemble arms or legs. This was a momentous transition, since the descendants of these creatures did indeed develop limbs and eventually crawled onto dry land. For a while, there were creatures that were part fish and part tetrapod (four-footed animal), living in the water but able to breathe air. Such confusing "amphibians" were soon making forays onto land and before long were spreading all over the world.

When organisms change, they are usually adapting to their changing environments. The best adapted members of a species thrive and go on to reproduce, whereas the less well adapted members struggle to survive. Over time, the results are evolution and extinction. Such evolutionary change may happen quite quickly, in some kind of adaptive leap, or it may be slow and gradual. Scientists think that the transition from fish to tetrapod was very gradual, while the sudden arrival of flying reptiles, at a later stage in this story, suggests a rapid burst of evolution. But we cannot be sure – perhaps we have simply not found the fossils of "in-between" creatures that would show how flying reptiles also evolved over a long period of time. The landscape onto which these first tetrapods crawled was unlike any seen upon the Earth before. The primitive plants of the Silurian period gave rise to plants with broad leaves, woody stems and roots. Some grew to heights of 18 m (60 ft) or more, so that they may have looked like modern trees. Forests had begun to cover areas of the Earth, and for the first time the land was shaded from the Sun by a canopy of leaves. Seed-bearing ferns, and mosses and swamp plants flourished in this new green world. More plants meant more food for the arthropods. Early wingless insects that ate rotting vegetation had appeared. There were now true spiders, too, seizing insects in their jaws and sucking out their life, while centipedes, scorpions and mites between them munched on plants, or one another.

But after more than 60 million years, this world, too, came to an end. The Devonian period also closed with a mass extinction of life, possibly as a result of cooling temperatures. Indeed, during the vast length of this age there were probably several such events in which unimaginable numbers of species vanished for ever. It is as if the Earth were some kind of creative laboratory, repeatedly testing for the life that is most enduring.

**ICHTHYOSTEGA'S FOOT**
The flipper-like shape of this tetrapod's fin, ending in seven small toes, shows that it evolved in water.

**OUT ON A LIMB**
The early tetrapod *Acanthostega* could breathe air, but its small limbs meant that it seldom ventured onto land. It spent most of its time in shallow water.

# The age *of* coal

*The Devonian was followed by the **Carboniferous** and **Permian** periods, which lasted some 106 million years. This time is also known as "the age of coal".*

THE EARTH'S TWO MAIN LANDMASSES, Gondwana and Laurentia, were now moving together. Florida was part of the southern supercontinent Gondwana, and California existed only in the shape of volcanic islands. The Carboniferous period witnessed great climatic contrasts. For a while, the northern supercontinent Laurentia sweltered close to the equator, but ice sheets gripped Gondwana as it crept across the South Pole. As climates changed and landmasses shifted, the sea level rose and fell. Its advance and retreat are marked in layers of rock. In cross-section, rock formed during this time looks rather like the layers of a cake, except that there are thousands of layers. The fossils of plants and animals are locked inside the rock, preserving

a record of the past. From this evidence, we know that the Carboniferous was a time in which huge tropical forests spread across the northern half of the globe. So much oxygen was released into the air by trees that the level of this vital gas rose to 35 per cent of the Earth's atmosphere, higher than at any time since (today, about 21 per cent of the atmosphere is oxygen). As we shall see, these vast quantities of oxygen meant that invertebrates, whose inefficient breathing mechanisms usually limit growth, could now evolve as giants.

The trees were giants, too. The mighty *Lepidodendron* and *Sigillaria*, colossal relatives of today's lowly clubmosses, reached heights of 50 m (160 ft) or more, dominating the swamp-like environment in which they grew. Tree ferns grew to heights of 8 m (26 ft). The plant life was luxuriant in this humid and shaded world of leaf and tree. Some trees grew straight and tall, as simple as any plant could be, but they were distinguished by the elegant arrangement of their leaves in the shapes of rings or spirals.

Shades upon shades of green were reflected in the brackish water of pools and lakes, but as yet no bright colours, because there were no flowers in the world. And the noises, too, were subdued. There were no calls or cries, only the dry scraping or the vague hum of huge insects.

**UNSTEADY GIANTS**
Swampy forest floors caused the giant clubmoss *Lepidodendron* to topple over easily. Today's swamp trees have broad supporting roots to keep them upright.

When these mighty trees and ferns eventually fell to the ground, their decaying tissues built up in layers as peat, a substance rather like dense, dark soil. Over many millions of years, the peat was compressed and fossilized into the black rock we know as coal. The coal beds of the world are our inheritance from the Carboniferous period, whose name literally means "coal-bearing". How curious to think that the energy that enabled the modern industrial world to emerge was drawn from these ancient origins. We are still dependent on our prehistoric past. Every age of the planet connects to what went before; the ancient past still helps us to live.

And what of the insects and other arthropods that flew around or crawled across these ancient trees? Some were the largest and strangest of their kind ever to have lived. There were, of course, cockroaches and woodlice, making their quiet way through the quiet earth as they would do for countless millions of years. But there were also giants in the arthropod world. In the shadows of the trees and ferns there lurked a spider of truly monstrous proportions. *Megarachne* had a leg span of more than 50 cm (20 in). Its fossil, found in Argentina, shows it to be the largest species of spider ever recorded. Its size probably meant that it preyed upon vertebrate creatures.

**COAL LEAF**
This elegant fern grew in the great forests of the Carboniferous. It fell into water-logged peat, which, over millions of years, was compressed into coal.

**MEGA SPIDER**
The Carboniferous spider *Megarachne* had a body the size of a small cat. It was twice the size of the largest spider in the world today, the Goliath Bird-Eating Spider, and almost three times the size of the tarantula shown here.

**ARTHROPODS GALORE**
Many new types of arthropod thrived in the humid world of the Carboniferous. This one, called *Graeophonus*, is an ancestor of today's whip spider.

One species of dragonfly had a wingspan of some 66 cm (26 in), which makes it the largest flying insect in the history of the Earth. Imagine such a thing flapping its way through the air towards you upon its stiff wings, with its antennae waving and its bulbous eyes swivelling as it hunts for prey. It is a thing out of a nightmare. Yet it is also a source of wonder, since it shows that land animals had now taken to the air. All insects' wings probably had the same origin, evolving from little gill plates raised as sails to help them skim across the surfaces of ancient ponds. Insect flight marked the land animals' first break from the surface of the Earth that nourished them, a triumph of biological engineering more complex than the technology of any modern space adventure and, more importantly, a triumph for the spirit of life itself.

This early dragonfly, named *Namurotypus*, lived in great swamp forests inhabited by creatures that would have seemed freakish and terrifying to

**FOOD TO GO**
*Namurotypus*, a giant Carboniferous dragonfly, used its strong legs to grab insects and eat as it flew. Today's dragonflies do the same, but have weaker legs.

**WESTLOTHIANA LIZZIAE**
This small Carboniferous tetrapod may have been a very early relative of the reptiles.

## Amniotic egg

The reptiles were among the first creatures to protect their offspring within a sealed structure called the amniotic egg. This advance allowed reptiles to colonize dry land, unlike amphibians, which had to remain near water where their eggs could be kept moist. Many later reptiles stopped laying eggs altogether and nourished their embryos internally. This gave the embryos even better protection.

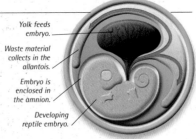

Yolk feeds embryo.

Waste material collects in the allantois.

Embryo is enclosed in the amnion.

Developing reptile embryo.

**Shell features**
The shell of an amniotic egg prevents the embryo inside from drying out on land. The yolk is the food store for the embryo, which is cushioned inside a sac called the amnion.

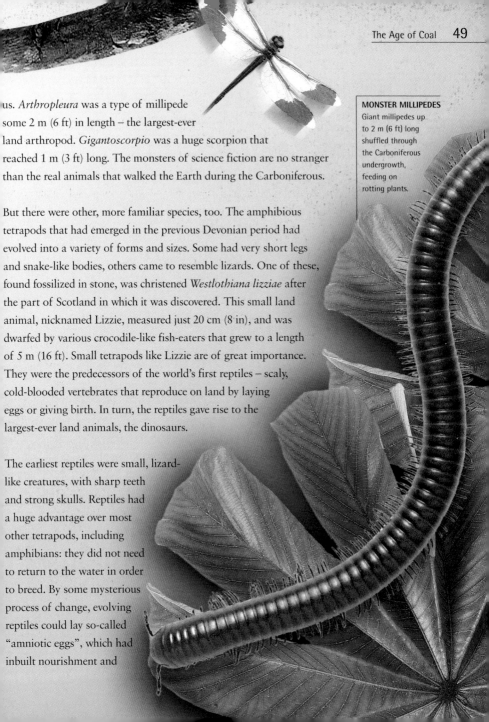

us. *Arthropleura* was a type of millipede some 2 m (6 ft) in length – the largest-ever land arthropod. *Gigantoscorpio* was a huge scorpion that reached 1 m (3 ft) long. The monsters of science fiction are no stranger than the real animals that walked the Earth during the Carboniferous.

But there were other, more familiar species, too. The amphibious tetrapods that had emerged in the previous Devonian period had evolved into a variety of forms and sizes. Some had very short legs and snake-like bodies, others came to resemble lizards. One of these, found fossilized in stone, was christened *Westlothiana lizziae* after the part of Scotland in which it was discovered. This small land animal, nicknamed Lizzie, measured just 20 cm (8 in), and was dwarfed by various crocodile-like fish-eaters that grew to a length of 5 m (16 ft). Small tetrapods like Lizzie are of great importance. They were the predecessors of the world's first reptiles – scaly, cold-blooded vertebrates that reproduce on land by laying eggs or giving birth. In turn, the reptiles gave rise to the largest-ever land animals, the dinosaurs.

The earliest reptiles were small, lizard-like creatures, with sharp teeth and strong skulls. Reptiles had a huge advantage over most other tetrapods, including amphibians: they did not need to return to the water in order to breed. By some mysterious process of change, evolving reptiles could lay so-called "amniotic eggs", which had inbuilt nourishment and

**MONSTER MILLIPEDES**
Giant millipedes up to 2 m (6 ft) long shuffled through the Carboniferous undergrowth, feeding on rotting plants.

tough, leathery skins or shells that allowed the unborn young to develop and then hatch out in dry surroundings. These special eggs meant that the first reptiles could spread and diversify away from water. There was one very early species of reptile called *Hylonomus*, or "forest mouse", which looked more like a tiny dragon than anything resembling a mouse. Palaeontologists (scientists who study fossil plants and animals) have found its bones in fossilized hollow tree-stumps in Nova Scotia, Canada. These little reptiles had either ventured there in search of prey and become trapped, or had taken refuge from the spread of wildfires. Their remains seem small and helpless compared with some of the monstrous arthropods that roamed the Carboniferous landscape, but they were the earliest known ancestors of one of the most enduring groups of vertebrates in the Earth's history. From these early reptiles would come crocodiles, dinosaurs and, eventually, birds. Birds are descended from reptiles whose scales had turned to feathers and whose front limbs had become wings.

**INSECT HUNTER**
Once its body temperature had warmed up in the morning sun, the tiny reptile *Hylonomus* could probably have darted very quickly after small arthropods, which it crushed and munched in its strong jaws.

Another form of egg-laying vertebrate also emerged in this period. The members of this group are called synapsids ("with arches") because of a skull hole behind each eye, which may have been a socket to house certain jaw muscles. Descendants of early synapsids developed fur and warm blood, giving rise to the first mammals – hairy, warm-blooded animals that produce milk to suckle their young. During the Carboniferous, however, the synapsids still resembled lizards and grew to a size of about 3.5 m (12 ft). Some had a huge fin, or sail, on their back. This may have played some part in communication with others of their kind, or perhaps the sail maintained the temperature of the body when it caught the rays of the Sun or the breath of the cool wind.

The ice returned in force at the end of the Carboniferous, and the world then entered the Permian period. This lasted for 42 million years, from

...00 to 248 million years ago. The Permian is named after the Perm region of the Ural Mountains, which now form a natural barrier between the European and Asian parts of Russia. These mountains were created by the shaping event of the Permian period. The vast landmasses of Gondwana and Laurentia collided with each other and with smaller continents such as Siberia, creating one great landmass that covered the world almost from pole to pole. This has been given the name Pangaea, which means "all of the Earth" in the ancient Greek language. It was the greatest continent in the world's history.

## COLD PHASE
The Carboniferous ended in a cold phase as the level of so-called greenhouse gases in the atmosphere fell. These gases trap heat and keep the planet warm. Their level rises or falls periodically.

In the southern regions of Pangaea, the glaciation that had marked the end of the Carboniferous period lingered. Great ice sheets covered what is now South America, Antarctica, Africa and Australia. This ice did not thaw until a further warming of the Earth occurred in the mid-Permian period. However, much of the central region of Pangaea, which lay across the equator, was so far from the sea that clouds could not reach it without evaporating, and so it consisted of nothing but desert. The luxuriant swamps of the Carboniferous gave way to great dry plains where very little life could survive. But many amphibians and reptiles thrived in the north of Pangaea, where conditions were damper and more humid.

## SUPERCONTINENT
Pangaea, a gigantic single continent, formed 250 million years ago. It slowly split into the landmasses

The shallow seas that surrounded Pangaea teemed with life, too. In the warm and brackish water there were many types of corals and snails, ammonites and crustaceans. We can only wonder at what strange creatures, still unknown to scientists, swam in the depths of one great sea, called the Tethys. That is one of the mysteries of this evolutionary history. There were millions of species at any one time upon the planet, and most of them must still be unknown. Buried underground are an estimated 500 million fossil species, but up to this date only a few hundred thousand species have been unearthed. Our ignorance of so much vanished life remains enormous. Even today, of the 10–30 million species possibly living on the Earth, most remain unnamed and unknown. So in our backward glance into the abyss of time, we have really seen very little. We are on the beach of life, and have so far picked up only a few stray shells and pebbles.

The great continent of Pangaea was so vast that there were patterns of distribution among both animals and plants. Scientists have discovered the leaves of the same extinct seed-fern, for example, in India and Antarctica, South Africa and South America. This was the first proof that these now widely separate landmasses were once all joined together. In the areas of harsher and drier climate within this supercontinent, amphibians were at a disadvantage to reptiles and synapsids, which as we have seen no longer needed to retreat into water to lay eggs. Both groups flourished, but the synapsids were more numerous at first, and accounted for about three-quarters of all four-legged land vertebrates. The fossil record of the Permian is filled with synapsids' bones and their distinctive teeth.

Synapsids began to spread from north to south as the climate of the period changed. Early synapsids are known as pelycosaurs and resembled large scaly lizards, with strong jaws and formidable fangs. The ferocious-looking pelycosaur *Dimetrodon* was one of first land animals capable of preying on creatures its own size – usually other, plant-eating pelycosaurs.

During the course of the Permian, pelycosaurs gradually evolved into more advanced creatures known as therapsids, which had a wider variety of body shapes and sizes. Permian therapsids included the land's first stout, four-legged herbivores (plant-eaters) as well as the big, powerful hunters that preyed upon them. Among them were the dicynodonts ("two dog teeth"), which looked a bit like pigs or hippopotamuses, with teeth designed for chewing plants. Another group of therapsids was the dinocephalians ("terrible heads"). Some of these huge-headed beasts possessed bizarre, horned structures on their heads. Interestingly, they had the erect hindlimbs of a mammal but the widely spread forelimbs of a reptile. This is an indication, perhaps, that different body parts on the same animal may evolve at different rates. The dinocephalians did

**FOSSIL PROOF**
These are the fossil remains of *Glossopteris*, a large seed-fern that grew in the southern parts of Pangaea. The discovery of its fossils all over the world was the first proof that today's widely separated continents were once part of a single landmass.

**SAIL-BACKED KILLER**
*Dimetrodon* probably kept cool in hot weather by turning its spectacular sail to face the breeze. At dawn, it may have warmed up by facing the sail towards the Sun. This may have helped the creature to be active in the early morning, while its prey was still cold and sluggish.

**LITTLE MESOSAURS**
During the Permian, these reptiles returned to live in water, probably because of the amount of prey to be found there. They evolved paddle-like tails, and webbed fingers and toes.

not survive the period, however, and left no descendants. But one group of therapsids – the carnivorous, dog-like cynodonts ("dog teeth") – was ultimately more successful. These fast-moving predators proliferated in the next great period, the Triassic.

The two main types of reptile were also established by this time: the diapsids ("two arches") and the anapsids ("without arches"). They are named according to the number of holes in the skull behind each eye socket – the conventional way of grouping reptiles. Diapsids include some extinct reptiles and some that are still alive today. Early forms in the Permian included lizard-like creatures, and at least one, *Coelurosauravus*, that glided on skin "wings". Anapsids, also known as "parareptiles", included small, lizard-like forms as well as much larger animals, some of them bristling with spikes and armour plates. The fearsome-looking *Scutosaurus* ("shield lizard"), for example, was a heavily built herbivore some 2.5 m (8 ft) long, with a huge, rounded body covered in bony horns and bumps. A sister group to the parareptiles were the little mesosaurs, or "middle lizards", which had, as it were, gone back along their evolutionary path and returned to the water.

**ANIMAL WITH GUTS**
*Scutosaurus'* bloated body housed enormous guts for digesting tough plant food. Its spikes and horns developed with age and may have been used in mating displays or fights.

Evolution does not always proceed in one direction, from simple to complex, from small to large, or from water to land. It may jump off and wander in a stray direction, it

**PERMIAN GLIDER**
The tree-dwelling reptile *Coelurosauravus* had long, bony rods on its back. These supported skin membranes that stretched out to form wings for gliding.

may decide to go downwards, it may stay where it is and refuse to climb upwards. Some scientists compare the process of evolution to a bush, with a thousand different branches growing in different but related directions. Plants and animals adapt to the pressures of competition or to changes in their environments. The example of the reptile returning to water is typical of the way evolution may lead in unexpected directions. Yet, at other times, the evidence suggests that evolution does indeed spring forwards. *Coelurosauravus* is unmistakably a winged reptile. It was, in essence, much like today's flying lizard. It could not have flown very far, and perhaps simply glided from tree to tree rather than embark on any ambitious aerial exercises, but it did fly. This is another extraordinary development in the history of the world. We could describe it as a "burst" of evolution.

At the end of the Permian period, about 248 million years ago, the Earth became silent. It was a time that witnessed the greatest of all extinctions in the world's history – a huge destruction of life, comprising 90 per cent of all species. It was the age of death itself. The oceans heated up, and 95 per cent of its living populations died. Key coral groups vanished. The trilobites, those tough little creatures that had survived for about 270 million years, completely disappeared. Seventy per cent of all land animals were also wiped away. It was a

**VOLCANIC UPHEAVAL**
Volcanoes played a major part in the Permian mass extinction. Eruptions buried vast areas of land beneath millions of cubic kilometres of lava, and blocked out the Sun's light with gas and dust.

**MARINE MASS DEATH**
Towards the end of the Permian, oxygen levels in sea water fell, possibly as a result of sluggish ocean circulation. This suffocated coral reefs and the thousands of different species that lived in them.

true catastrophe for the planet. Scientists have not identified any one cause for this mass graveyard, although climate changes must have played a part. The ocean retreated from the shorelines of Pangaea and the shallow inland seas dried up, leaving much marine life stranded. There was also massive volcanic activity during this period, forming dense clouds of dust and carbon dioxide gas. Heat trapped beneath this blanket of cloud steadily warmed up the surface of the planet. The rising temperatures may even have triggered the sudden, massive release of a gas called methane hydrate from the seabed, which would have asphyxiated marine life. In any event, the oxygen levels in the seas dropped. The violent impacts of large meteorites, which may have struck at this time, would have made conditions worse, sending tsunamis (giant sea waves) around the world. There are, in truth, many possible explanations, and it seems likely that all – or most – of them contributed to the extinction of life.

This has become a pattern in the Earth's history. In the last 500 million years

**GIANT SEA WAVES**
Tsunamis are giant sea waves, caused by earthquakes or meteorites. They travel at the speed of a jet aircraft, but slow down as they reach land.

there have been 54 extinction events, which suggests that this globe is indeed a dangerous place to inhabit. Certain mass extinctions were the direct result of meteorite strikes. There are 30 craters in the world that are larger than 10 km (6 miles) wide. The meteorites that caused these would have been fearsome things. The effects upon life would also have been catastrophic. However, most mass extinctions stem from events taking place within the planet. Temperature fluctuations in the molten outer core trigger shudders and sighs in the deep structures of the Earth. As a result, the tectonic plates keep shifting, repositioning landmasses, throwing up mountain chains, and causing vast volumes of molten rock and gas to spew from volcanoes. From time to time, these global upheavals, combined with periodic changes in the Earth's path around the Sun, make the planet heat up or freeze. Today, the Earth is still in one of its "ice" phases; but that will one day come to an end, and the polar ice caps will be considered the miracle of a past age.

The history of the Earth could be said to be the history of the disappeared. The footsteps of Permian reptiles found in desert sand are unique; they can never be formed again. Imagine the loneliness of the last creature of its kind upon the Earth, whose death will extinguish its species forever. There may, however, be one note of comfort in this chronicle of continual change. Certain species have survived. There seems to be some lasting structure of life that is maintained in this roll call of life and death. The vertebrates, for example, have survived all 54 extinction events and prosper still.

**WALKING TO EXTINCTION**
These lone, fossilized footprints were made by a Permian reptile more than 250 million years ago. Reptile groups were severely reduced in numbers by the extinction events that marked the end of the Permian period.

HADEAN AEON                                              ARCHAEAN AEON

# CHAPTER SIX

# The rule *of the* reptiles

*In the Permian period,
many species flourished and
died, but they were replaced
in the Triassic period by
wonderful new creatures.*

WITH THE BEGINNING of the Triassic period, the Palaeozoic era, or "Age of Ancient Life", came to an end after 300 million years. There now began a new era, the Mesozoic, or "Age of Middle Life". We divide the 180 million years of the Mesozoic era into three distinct periods – the Triassic, the Jurassic and

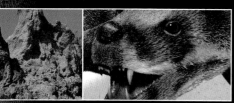

the Cretaceous. These were the periods when reptiles ruled the Earth. The main group of reptiles at this time were the archosaurs, which included the most famous of all prehistoric creatures, the dinosaurs. The great landmass of Pangaea was still the dominant geographical fact of the Triassic, although it is possible to see the vague outlines of Africa, the Americas and Asia glimmering through the united mass of land.

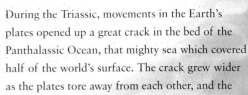

During the Triassic, movements in the Earth's plates opened up a great crack in the bed of the Panthalassic Ocean, that mighty sea which covered half of the world's surface. The crack grew wider as the plates tore away from each other, and the gap was continually filled by hot lava oozing up from the molten mantle below. The moving plates carried Pangaea slowly northwards, causing the regions that crossed the equator to became hotter and drier. In such a long expanse of time – the Triassic period lasted from 248 to 206 million years ago – there were great changes in climate

**MARINE ARCHOSAUR**
*Nothosaurus* was an amphibious, long-necked predator with numerous fang-like teeth. It lived mainly in the Triassic seas but may have rested and bred on dry land, much like today's seals.

and in geography. The sea level rose and fell, and the temperature also varied, although it is clear that the Earth was a warmer place than it is today. New forms of coral grew in the warm, sun-dappled seas, harbouring many varieties of bony fishes. Perfect fossils of these creatures have been found; they seem to be swimming in the stone. The varieties of cephalopod and mollusc exploded once more, and out of two or three species a hundred more evolved. There were sea snails and ammonites, all of them creating a sea life of enormous diversity.

Many reptiles took to the water once again, perhaps because of the amount of prey that they could capture. Prominent among these were the nothosaurs and ichthyosaurs. They are not related to dinosaurs, although some people have mistakenly classified them as dinosaurs of the ocean. Nothosaurs could grow to 3 m (10 ft) in length, and with their long necks and large flippers glided swiftly through the Triassic waters. Some of the ichthyosaurs grew to 23 m (75 ft). Despite being so

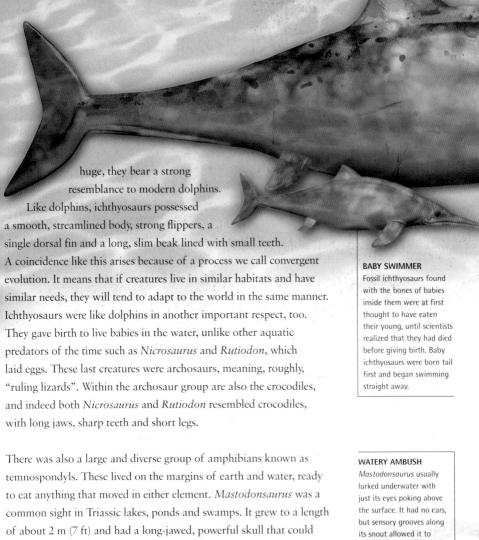

huge, they bear a strong resemblance to modern dolphins. Like dolphins, ichthyosaurs possessed a smooth, streamlined body, strong flippers, a single dorsal fin and a long, slim beak lined with small teeth. A coincidence like this arises because of a process we call convergent evolution. It means that if creatures live in similar habitats and have similar needs, they will tend to adapt to the world in the same manner. Ichthyosaurs were like dolphins in another important respect, too. They gave birth to live babies in the water, unlike other aquatic predators of the time such as *Nicrosaurus* and *Rutiodon*, which laid eggs. These last creatures were archosaurs, meaning, roughly, "ruling lizards". Within the archosaur group are also the crocodiles, and indeed both *Nicrosaurus* and *Rutiodon* resembled crocodiles, with long jaws, sharp teeth and short legs.

There was also a large and diverse group of amphibians known as temnospondyls. These lived on the margins of earth and water, ready to eat anything that moved in either element. *Mastodonsaurus* was a common sight in Triassic lakes, ponds and swamps. It grew to a length of about 2 m (7 ft) and had a long-jawed, powerful skull that could snatch fishes as well as small land-living animals.

It was the archosaurs, however, that became dominant during the Triassic. Prominent among them were large, four-footed animals called aetosaurs, which were covered in scales like heavy armour.

**BABY SWIMMER**
Fossil ichthyosaurs found with the bones of babies inside them were at first thought to have eaten their young, until scientists realized that they had died before giving birth. Baby ichthyosaurs were born tail first and began swimming straight away.

**WATERY AMBUSH**
*Mastodonsaurus* usually lurked underwater with just its eyes poking above the surface. It had no ears, but sensory grooves along its snout allowed it to "hear" vibrations made in the water by its prey.

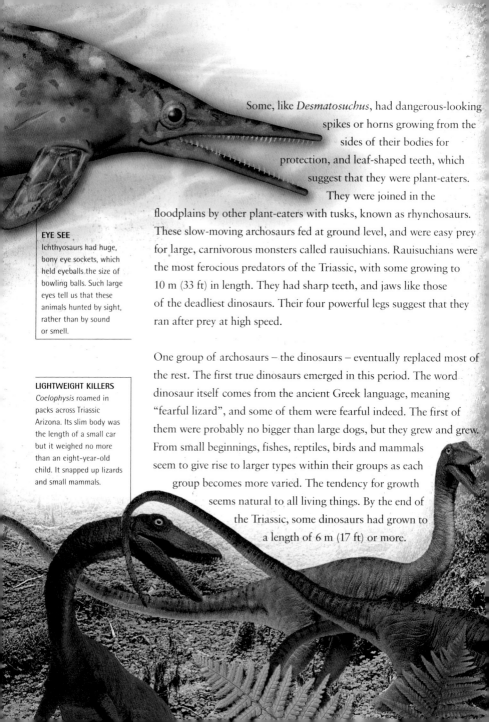

Some, like *Desmatosuchus*, had dangerous-looking spikes or horns growing from the sides of their bodies for protection, and leaf-shaped teeth, which suggest that they were plant-eaters. They were joined in the floodplains by other plant-eaters with tusks, known as rhynchosaurs. These slow-moving archosaurs fed at ground level, and were easy prey for large, carnivorous monsters called rauisuchians. Rauisuchians were the most ferocious predators of the Triassic, with some growing to 10 m (33 ft) in length. They had sharp teeth, and jaws like those of the deadliest dinosaurs. Their four powerful legs suggest that they ran after prey at high speed.

One group of archosaurs – the dinosaurs – eventually replaced most of the rest. The first true dinosaurs emerged in this period. The word dinosaur itself comes from the ancient Greek language, meaning "fearful lizard", and some of them were fearful indeed. The first of them were probably no bigger than large dogs, but they grew and grew. From small beginnings, fishes, reptiles, birds and mammals seem to give rise to larger types within their groups as each group becomes more varied. The tendency for growth seems natural to all living things. By the end of the Triassic, some dinosaurs had grown to a length of 6 m (17 ft) or more.

**EYE SEE**
Ichthyosaurs had huge, bony eye sockets, which held eyeballs the size of bowling balls. Such large eyes tell us that these animals hunted by sight, rather than by sound or smell.

**LIGHTWEIGHT KILLERS**
*Coelophysis* roamed in packs across Triassic Arizona. Its slim body was the length of a small car but it weighed no more than an eight-year-old child. It snapped up lizards and small mammals.

They would have strode or plodded across the Earth. Some were two-legged, others four-legged, but all walked on their toes, or "fingers" and toes, using their tails to balance.

Largest of the early dinosaurs were the long-necked, plant-eating prosauropods, which were mostly four-legged. These were probably the first vertebrates tall enough to graze on tree leaves while standing on the ground. They were also the first dinosaurs to grow as heavy as today's elephants.

Among the smaller dinosaurs was an early theropod, or carnivorous dinosaur, known as *Coelophysis*, which may have hunted in packs like dogs. They were not very large, but they must have been very fierce. Perhaps now and then they even ate each other. The fossils of young *Coelophysis* have been found apparently in the stomachs of adults.

**ANIMAL CANNIBALS**
Tiny bones inside the ribcage of this fossil *Coelophysis* show that its last meal had been one of its own kind – a baby *Coelophysis*. Adults probably ate any creature small enough to swallow. Some living reptiles, such as crocodiles, do the same.

## From cynodont to mammal

The jaw bones of *Thrinaxodon*, a cynodont, illustrate a key "middle stage" along the evolutionary path that leads from early synapsids, such as *Dimetrodon*, to modern mammals. Over time, jaw bones shrank so that the entire lower jaw consisted of a large dentary bone. The jaw's hinge bones gradually moved inside the skull to form the mammal's middle-ear bones – no longer used for biting but for hearing. They transmit sound waves as vibrations to the inner ear.

**Thrinaxodon skull**
Dentary bone is large and hinge bones are crowded to the back of the jaw where the ear drum is located.

Dentary bone

Hinge bones

**Dimetrodon skull**
Jaw contains smaller dentary bone, and a large group of hinge bones. Ear is located behind the jaw.

Dentary bone

Hinge bones

Most intriguing, however, are the flying reptiles. These were creatures with fearsome jaws and teeth and the unmistakeable framework of wings. There were other reptiles that glided, with long legs stretched out behind them. But the best known are the pterosaurs. These flying reptiles had membranes of skin stretching from the long fourth finger of each hand to the main body. They had long tails, too, which helped to stabilize their flight. They had big skulls; if you had faced one swooping down upon you, you would have seen a great beak and large, bulging eyes. Their wingspan varied, but the largest were more than 2.5 m (8 ft) across. With their sharp teeth, however, they might have seemed like flying dinosaurs.

Besides the reptiles were the synapsids, which as we have seen emerged in the Carboniferous. Some of them, the cynodonts, now looked like dogs more than 1 m (3 ft) in length, with pointed canine teeth. They were all probably covered with hair, and small versions were the direct ancestors of the most important new arrivals in the world – the mammals. One of the earliest mammals resembled a shrew, complete with long, mobile snout. It made burrows in the ground, and was nocturnal. In a dangerous world, it was probably safer for these little furry animals to emerge at night than in the daytime. No doubt these early mammals lived upon the insect life of the Triassic, among which were beetles and cockroaches directly related to the insects of our own time. The survival of insects is one of the miracles of the planet, a symbol of the persistence of life in extreme circumstances.

In the Triassic, the first colonies, or cities, of termites appeared. These tiny creatures flourished by

swamps and by lagoons, in enormous forests of conifers and in clumps of monkey-puzzle trees. There were other familiar creatures in this primeval landscape, too. A creature much like a frog first emerged in the Triassic. The crocodiles' ancestors made their first appearance. The turtles arrived, and have visited beaches to lay their eggs ever since, together with the king crabs. These animals all survived yet another extinction that marked the end of the Triassic period – an extinction in which, once again, many forms of marine and land life completely vanished. The Triassic, which had lasted for some 42 million years, was now replaced by the more famous Jurassic.

**COLONIAL CITIES**
During the Triassic, termites formed enormous "cities" in which different groups performed specialized tasks to help the colony thrive, much like today's termites.

# CHAPTER SEVEN

# World *of* giants

*The **Jurassic** period is named after the Jura mountains in France and Switzerland, where certain rock formations date from that distant time.*

THIS WAS A PERIOD THAT LASTED for some 64 million years, from 206 to 142 million years ago. It was a time when the Earth's climate was generally warm and the polar ice caps melted away. The success of the *Jurassic Park* films means that the period itself probably needs no introduction. Yet it is more varied and more surprising than even the films themselves revealed. Pangaea, the great landmass of the world, began its slow break-up, and the Atlantic Ocean began to fill the widening gap between Africa and South America. If you look at these two great continents on a map, you can see clearly how they were once joined together like the pieces from a giant jigsaw puzzle. The relentless movement of the tectonic plates over the ages has

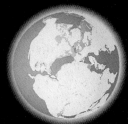

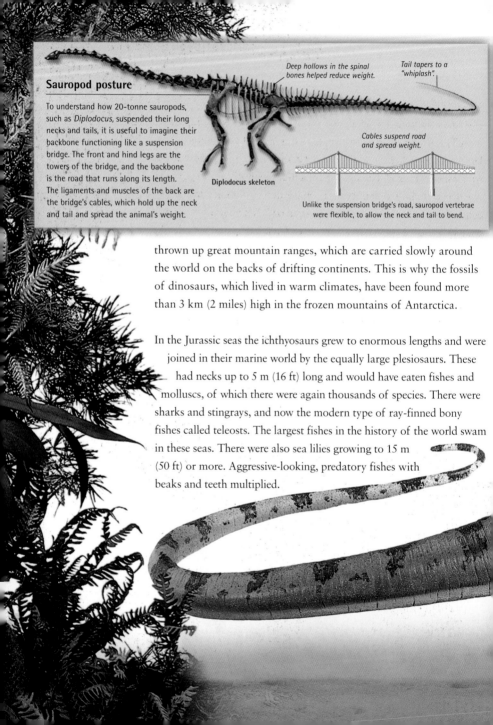

## Sauropod posture

To understand how 20-tonne sauropods, such as *Diplodocus*, suspended their long necks and tails, it is useful to imagine their backbone functioning like a suspension bridge. The front and hind legs are the towers of the bridge, and the backbone is the road that runs along its length. The ligaments and muscles of the back are the bridge's cables, which hold up the neck and tail and spread the animal's weight.

Deep hollows in the spinal bones helped reduce weight.

Tail tapers to a "whiplash".

Diplodocus skeleton

Cables suspend road and spread weight.

Unlike the suspension bridge's road, sauropod vertebrae were flexible, to allow the neck and tail to bend.

thrown up great mountain ranges, which are carried slowly around the world on the backs of drifting continents. This is why the fossils of dinosaurs, which lived in warm climates, have been found more than 3 km (2 miles) high in the frozen mountains of Antarctica.

In the Jurassic seas the ichthyosaurs grew to enormous lengths and were joined in their marine world by the equally large plesiosaurs. These had necks up to 5 m (16 ft) long and would have eaten fishes and molluscs, of which there were again thousands of species. There were sharks and stingrays, and now the modern type of ray-finned bony fishes called teleosts. The largest fishes in the history of the world swam in these seas. There were also sea lilies growing to 15 m (50 ft) or more. Aggressive-looking, predatory fishes with beaks and teeth multiplied.

Upon the Jurassic Earth there were shallow inland seas and tropical vegetation. While some of the inner regions of Pangaea must have remained dry – barren plains of sand and sand dunes – the largest proportion of land was clothed in forests and jungles, rivers and streams, swamps and marshes. The plentiful supply of lush vegetation, together with the year-round warm temperatures, provided ideal conditions for the dinosaurs, which spread rapidly and evolved into a wide variety of shapes and sizes. It is worth reminding ourselves that by Jurassic times the sheer diversity and amount of life would have been astounding. It is easy to imagine a peaceful, undisturbed forest with only the bellows of a *Diplodocus* in the distance, but in fact the Earth was probably teeming with animals. Some of the largest-ever dinosaurs lived in the Jurassic period, standing taller than five-storey houses. Others were no more than half a metre or so in length and scuttled across the land at great speed.

*Diplodocus* reached about 27 m (89 ft) in length – longer than three red London buses – with four massively built legs, a long slender neck and a tapering tail. It was a plant-eater, but

**LONG NECK**
*Diplodocus*'s neck gave it an astoundingly long reach. Some scientists think that this animal could even rear up on its hind legs in order to reach the tree tops or to bring its stubby "hands" down on an attacker.

**MONSTER MEAT-EATER**
*Megalosaurus* was named in 1824 after the discovery of its gruesome fanged jawbone. It had a large head, thick neck and powerful legs. Its feet and hands each bore three murderously long, sharp claws.

**CREST POSTURING**
*Dilophosaurus's* two wafer-thin head crests were probably used for display. By nodding his head up and down while standing sideways, a male would have looked bigger and more dangerous.

it probably could not have raised its great neck very high and would instead have munched on low-lying ferns. There was one dinosaur of the same family that has been suitably named *Seismosaurus*, or "earth-shaking lizard". It grew to an incredible length of 34 m (110 ft) and weighed more than 30 tonnes. These monsters, known as sauropods, roamed the forests of the Jurassic, perhaps calling to each other with some cry that has never since been heard on sea or land. That is one aspect of these times that is generally ignored: since life had moved from the sea to the land, the Earth was no longer silent. At least some of the dinosaurs are likely to have evolved simple means of communicating with one another – cries of anger or of alarm, of battle or of mating. Besides the rustle of insects, there would now be a thousand other voices echoing beneath the canopies of the forests.

Among them would have been that of *Brachiosaurus*, or "arm lizard", another sauropod that thrived during the Jurassic. It was given that name because of its great front limbs, although its hind limbs were massive, too. Its thigh bone was over 2 m (6 ft) in length. This was another plant-eater with a gigantic neck, and it grew to a length of 25 m (82 ft). A human being would have been dwarfed by its legs alone, which stood like great pillars of flesh and bone.

In the early Jurassic, there were carnivorous dinosaurs such as *Dilophosaurus*, meaning "two ridge lizard" after the two crests on its skull. The purpose of these ridges is not known, except that they might have been some form of display to help individuals spot others of their kind, or to frighten away rivals. *Dilophosaurus* was part of a varied group of theropods known as ceratosaurs, or "horned lizards", some of which reached a length of 7 m (23 ft).

And then there were the monster meat-eaters. The fossilized remains of *Megalosaurus*, or "big lizard", were among the first of any

**COMPSOGNATHUS**
This small predator was a coelurosaur ("hollow-tailed lizard"), a new group of theropods that eventually gave rise to the mighty tyrannosaurs. It lived on warm islands, hunting insects and scavenging on creatures washed up on the shore.

dinosaur to be studied, and in the early 19th century they generated an obsession with the strange "lizards" of the prehistoric past. *Megalosaurus* was a predator, and a tetanuran ("stiff-tailed") theropod. Like the early dinosaurs, it walked on the toes of its hind feet; the three claw-tipped fingers of each hand extended to capture its prey. There were many variations on this type of hunting machine, some of them smaller and faster, some larger and more ponderous. Among these were the great meat-eating dinosaurs called allosaurs, which used their upper jaws as axes to chop down upon their big plant-eating prey.

*Stegosaurus* was one likely victim of the allosaurs, despite the great bony plates sticking up from its back. Its fearsome appearance is misleading: the plates were probably used to control the temperature of its body. Its hide was thick and tough, its throat was protected by studs made out of bone, while its tail bore four great spikes to ward off attack from the carnivores. The armour of the stegosaur gives us some idea of the dangerous world the dinosaurs inhabited.

That is why, when you see dinosaurs in pictures or at exhibitions, they are often shown in attitudes of attack or defence. The hunters' jaws are normally opened to reveal rows of dagger-like teeth, and their claws stick out aggressively

**HEAVY DEFENCES**
The awesome plates on *Stegosaurus*'s back were probably not part of its defences but for body temperature control. The animal was well protected by a mace-like tail that ended in long spikes, and studs that covered its neck like chain-mail.

In truth, however, this is only half the story of the dinosaurs. In recent years, it has become clear to scientists that many species and groups lived a communal and family life. Plant-eaters herded together for safety and support. Some built communal nests, with their eggs gathered together in a place of safety, and certain theropods evidently settled down to brood over their unborn young like a mothering bird. The instincts for care and protection must have been strong. One creature of the Cretaceous period (which followed the Jurassic) has been found in a posture that suggests she was protecting her eggs from some imminent catastrophe. An avalanche of rain-sodden sand most likely overwhelmed her and the eggs, helping to create fossils that are now stone memorials of an infinitely remote time. Misnamed *Oviraptor* ("egg thief"), this nesting dinosaur was covered with feathers.

A feathered theropod must have been an amazing sight – particularly if its feathers were brightly coloured. Feathers were used to protect young, but they served mainly to prevent loss of body heat from what was probably a warm-blooded animal. And here is a miracle – from some feathered dinosaur there emerged the first bird.

The oldest known bird is called *Archaeopteryx* ("ancient wing"), which lived about 150 million years ago. This creature had the

**GOOD FLYER**
Although primitive, the Jurassic pterosaur *Dimorphodon* had large eyes and good balance, which suggests that it was a sophisticated flyer.

**EGG SHAPES AND SIZES**
There were many types of dinosaur eggs, ranging from "cannonballs" to "long loaves" (seen here) to tiny eggs that would fit in your hand.

head, hands, legs and bony tail structure of a small theropod dinosaur, but also wings and tail feathers that enabled it to fly. It had long, sprinter's shins, and large bright eyes to observe its prey. It was about the size of a crow or a magpie. Originally, palaeontologists believed that this bird climbed the trunks of the trees, using its large claws to grip, and then glided to catch small animals or insects. But it now seems possible that *Archaeopteryx* took off by running along the ground. Feathered creatures like this were the ancestors of all today's birds.

The earliest birds such as *Archaeopteryx* had teeth, as did another group of vertebrates populating the Jurassic air – the flying reptiles called pterosaurs. Some pterosaurs eventually achieved a wingspan of 12 m (40 ft) and were the size of a small aeroplane. Others were very small, no more than the size of an average sparrow. Pterosaurs had wings covered with skin, which were more vulnerable to damage than the feathered wings of birds. This is one reason why in time birds came to dominate the skies.

So the Jurassic period was indeed one of creative innovation and growth. Perhaps it is not surprising, then, that it became the subject of so many film adventures. In fact, the Jurassic has been the starting point for many other legends of the past. When a young Englishwoman in the early 19th century, Mary Anning, found ammonites in the rocks of

**SHORT FLIGHT**
*Archaeopteryx* may have run after insects and leapt to catch them in mid-air, staying aloft by flapping its wings. But this bird did not fly far. Its small breastbone suggests that its flapping muscles were weak.

**STONE FEATHERS**
This famous fossil *Archaeopteryx*, with feathers, convinced many scientists that birds are a type of dinosaur that learned to fly.

Lyme Regis, in south-west England, she sparked off a fossil craze. Soon, the remains of the ichthyosaurs and plesiosaurs that had prowled the Jurassic seas were uncovered, and at once there grew a fascination with these "monsters" of the deep. Many engravings were produced by artists portraying a nightmare world inhabited by unearthly creatures. They created an imaginary Earth like the makers of the films.

Dinosaur fossils and others have also been at the root of some strange superstitions. People once thought them to be representations of the devil or the remains of creatures drowned in the Biblical flood. They inspired myths and legends. In Greek mythology, the story of the one-eyed giant, Polyphemus, is probably based upon the finding of a fossil. The rumours of dragons and flying serpents, very common in the medieval period, were probably based on the discovery of rocks in which the shapes of dinosaurs and pterosaurs were embedded. The unearthing of petrified remains no doubt started the belief that there were divine beings who could turn a living creature into stone. In the 16th and 17th centuries, it was also believed that fossils were caused by natural forces in the ground itself – that they had, in some bizarre manner, been originally created in that form.

**DRAGON BELIEFS**
Old beliefs in dragons and sea serpents may have arisen from fossil dinosaur finds.

By the middle of the 19th century, however, most people accepted that the fossils were the remains of creatures long extinct. Imagine what an extraordinary leap of the imagination that required: the Earth was so old that monstrous creatures had once walked upon it but had now vanished. The Earth once had no human beings. It was a different kind of planet from the one we recognize today.

**DINOSAUR SCIENCE**
People have been unearthing fossil dinosaurs, such as this *Heterodontosaurus*, for thousands of years, but only in the 19th century did scientists begin to study them seriously. The term "dinosaur" ("terrible lizard") was coined by British palaeontologist Richard Owen in 1842.

# CHAPTER EIGHT

# Dinosaurs
# diversify

*The Earth now entered the next
great period of its history, the*
**Cretaceous**. *It is named after
chalk created from the tiny fossils
of organisms known as coccoliths.*

CRETACEOUS ITSELF MEANS "of the nature of chalk".
The chalk we use to write on blackboards is
made of marine creatures that existed more than
65 million years ago. It is one of the most direct, and yet
one of the most strange, reminders of prehistoric life. One
other example may be mentioned here. The modern world
depends upon oil, and much of that
oil formed from plankton that lived
in warm seas during the Cretaceous
period. When these tiny organisms
died, they were slowly buried
beneath the seabed and eventually
became trapped in rocks. Their decayed remains turned
gradually to black crude oil. The greatest fuel of the
modern age has been granted to us by the activity of
minuscule creatures from the distant past.

The Cretaceous period lasted from 142 to 65 million years ago — an age of some 77 million years. This was the last age of the dinosaurs. In their final period the dinosaurs grew ever more diverse and strange. This was partly the result of geological change. In the Cretaceous, the vast areas of Pangaea were finally split open into the recognizable continents, while great oceans formed between the different landmasses. North America and Europe began to draw apart, Africa and South America diverged, and the Atlantic Ocean expanded to fill the space between them. India remained an island, but China had fully emerged from the sea. Australia and Antarctica were still joined together, but an ocean began to form between them during the late Cretaceous, eventually to leave Antarctica in the magnificent polar isolation it still enjoys. The movement of the Earth's tectonic plates also caused long periods of volcanic activity. At certain times, the western coasts of the Americas would have been infernos of gas, volcanic dust and lava.

**VOLCANIC INFERNOS**
Water boils as lava flows into the sea around Hawaii. At various times during the Cretaceous, the western coasts of the Americas resembled scenes like this.

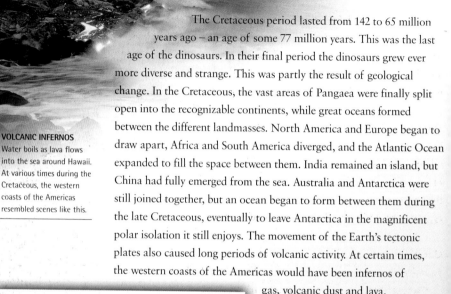

## Bird hips or lizard hips?

Dinosaurs are classified into one of two main groups, according to the structure of the pelvis (hip bones). These groups are the saurischian (lizard-hipped) and ornithischian (bird-hipped) dinosaurs. Confusingly, birds evolved from lizard-hipped dinosaurs.

**Lizard-hipped**
Most lizard-hipped dinosaurs had a forward-pointing pubis bone similar to a lizard's. The group included plant-eaters as well as carnivores.

Pubis bone

Gallimimus

**Bird-hipped**
Bird-hipped dinosaurs had a pubis bone that pointed backwards like a bird's. All were plant-eaters.

Pubis bone

Hypsilophodon

As the old supercontinent broke up and its pieces drifted apart, plant and animal life began to diversify according to the conditions of each separate terrain. The landscapes of these regions became quite different from each other. At various times, a vast floodplain lay where southern England is now; a sea stretching from north to south split North America in two; and deserts gripped the heart of Asia.

When the Cretaceous began, the dinosaurs had already existed for some 88 million years, and throughout the

period they were still the land's dominant animals. By the end of it, the dinosaurs had persisted in various forms for about 165 million years. Modern humans, or *Homo sapiens*, have not yet lasted one quarter of a million years. Our species will have to endure 660 times as long before it can claim to have had the staying power of the dinosaurs.

During the dinosaurs' last great phase of development, a tremendous variety of different species emerged. All of them belonged to one of two main groups: the saurischian ("lizard-hipped") dinosaurs and the ornithischian ("bird-hipped") dinosaurs, first defined by which way their pubic bones were angled. Adult dinosaurs in both groups laid eggs in nests, and probably helped to hatch and feed their young.

One of the strangest bird-hipped dinosaurs from the early Cretaceous period was *Psittacosaurus* ("parrot lizard"), whose skull resembled that of a parrot. The rest of its body was more like that of a lizard but with long hind legs. This harmless plant-eater would have been able to run quite fast to escape predators, which is perhaps one reason why its kind survived for more than 40 million years.

The theropods were an extremely varied group of lizard-hipped dinosaurs that produced some amazing bird-like forms. *Caudipteryx* ("tail feather") was covered with feathers. This dinosaur rather resembled a turkey, and probably pecked up seeds and

**DINOTURKEY**
With its beak and feathers, *Caudipteryx* resembled a flightless bird. However, its teeth and clawed hands suggest that this dinosaur was probably not in the process of evolving into a bird.

ground them with swallowed stones inside its stomach. Its long legs enabled it to run very fast. Another bird-like, feathered theropod is known as *Deinonychus*, or "terrible claw". This was a fearsome creature indeed, up to 3 m (10 ft) long, with sharp-toothed jaws and a huge, sickle-shaped claw on either foot, used for slashing downwards. A related species called *Velociraptor*, or "quick robber", was a hunter whose jaws bristled with blade-like fangs. It quite likely sprouted both hair-like, feathery filaments for warmth and long feathers for display.

**FEATHERED PREDATOR**
*Velociraptor* had several bird-like features. Recent evidence suggests that it was feathered, and it may even have folded its arms sideways, like wings.

Some of the most bird-like theropods are known as "bird mimic" dinosaurs, and remind us of flightless, long-legged birds such as ostriches. The largest of them, *Gallimimus*, or "chicken mimic", was 6 m (19.5 ft) long. It had a long neck like an ostrich, a bird-like beak, long arms with clawed fingers, and a long, bony tail.

We can only guess at the colour of all these dinosaurs. It is possible that their skin or feathers were arrayed in bright shades of blue, yellow and red, adding brilliancy to the Cretaceous landscape. Or perhaps they had camouflage colouration so that they might blend in with

**OSTRICH LEGS**
*Gallimimus* probably ran like an ostrich, lifting its legs in high strides. Unlike an ostrich, though, it also had a long, bony tail that kept it balanced.

the browns and greens of the primeval forests. There seems no reason to doubt that such natural protection had already developed by this time.

The main enemies of dinosaurs were other dinosaurs, and fights between them could be ferocious. Two fossils discovered in the Mongolian desert reveal what happened in one deadly struggle for survival. A *Velociraptor* had attacked a plant-eater known as *Protoceratops*, and was gripping its head while the herbivore had grasped its attacker with its beak. A sudden sandstorm had smothered them in the moment of their pitched battle, and they died gripping each other in a never-ending embrace. In some ways, these fossils are more meaningful than the most beautiful statue, because they are the sculptures of a silent and invisible past. They are true images of a lost world.

Protoceratops grabs attacker with beak.

Velociraptor grasps victim's snout and kicks with clawed feet.

Some dinosaurs may have fought others of their own species at times. *Pachycephalosaurus* males had a thick skull, probably for head-butting their rivals during the breeding season, just as today's bighorn rams do in the Rocky Mountains of the United States.

Strange though it appeared, the skull of *Pachycephalosaurus* looked no odder than the crested heads of the hadrosaurs, better known as "duck-billed dinosaurs" because of their broad, toothless beaks. Some had bizarre hollow structures upon the tops of their heads, which may have magnified the sound of their low-pitched bellows – perhaps to warn the herd of danger. These peaceful-looking

**DEADLY EMBRACE**
Even a vicious theropod like *Velociraptor* ran a risk when attacking a sturdily built plant-eater like *Protoceratops* – as these tangled fossils show. The theropod could not struggle free from its victim's bite, despite slashing downwards with deadly clawed feet.

**ROAD RUNNERS**
The tall, athletic *Gallimimus* might have sprinted as fast as 80 kph (50 mph) – faster than the fastest racehorse.

herbivores reached a length of 12 m (40 ft). Stranger still was the awkward beast known as *Therizinosaurus*, or "scythe lizard". It had a horse-like head, a long neck and plodded along on two long, heavy legs, but its short, stubby arms were equipped with extraordinary claws more than 60 cm (24 in) in length.

Other Cretaceous dinosaurs that sported extraordinary headgear included the plant-eating group known as ceratopsians, of which *Triceratops* is perhaps the best known. These had various combinations of horns on their faces and great frills of bone behind their heads. The horns made for superb defensive weapons, and the prominent frills were probably used for display.

The most famous dinosaurs of the Cretaceous, however, are *Iguanodon* and *Tyrannosaurus rex*. *Iguanodon* was a large herbivore, reaching a length of 9 m (30 ft). It walked on all fours, although it could rear up on its hind legs to reach the leaves of tall trees. On each thumb grew a spike that might have been used both for attack and for defence. The footprints and body-prints of *Iguanodon* have been found fossilized in lake deposits of the period, suggesting that like a present-day rhinoceros it enjoyed wallowing in mud. The number and closeness of fossilized prints also suggest that these animals wandered together in herds.

*Tyrannosaurus rex*, whose name means "king of the tyrant lizards", was an altogether more formidable animal. It had a great head and massive jaws, opening to reveal an array of thick, sharp teeth. Its mouth could have swallowed a human being in one savage movement. It is extraordinary that such a massive animal

## Hadrosaur crests

Hadrosaur crests housed strange cavities that may have been used to amplify sound signals to the herd. The type of sound varied depending on the crest shape. Low-frequency sounds carry over a great distance, and it would have been difficult for a predator to tell the direction from which they came.

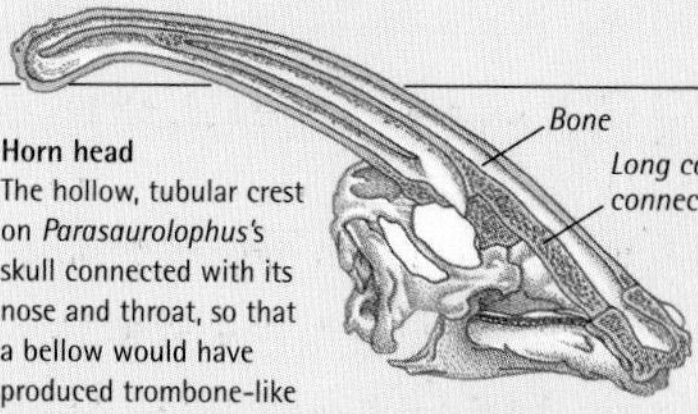

**Horn head**
The hollow, tubular crest on *Parasaurolophus*'s skull connected with its nose and throat, so that a bellow would have produced trombone-like honking noises. Trumpeting to each other may have been part of these animals' social behaviour.

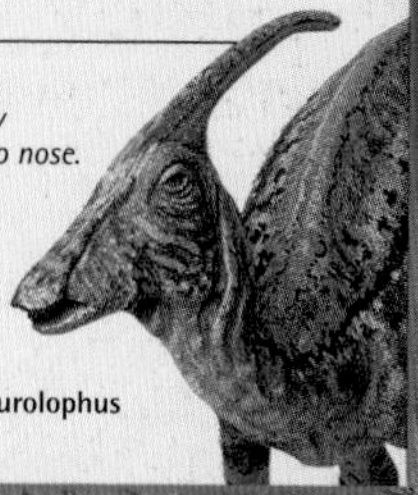

Bone

Long cavity connects to nose.

Parasaurolophus

Therizinosaurus
("scythe lizard")

Iguanodon
("iguana tooth")

walked on the three toes of its hind feet, an arrangement that perhaps allowed it to chase after its prey at surprisingly high speeds. Its arms were tiny but muscular, and each two-fingered hand ended in curling claws. These stubby arms were too small to grapple with prey, or bring food to the beast's mouth. They appear to be quite without use, as if in an evolutionary process of shrivelling away. Perhaps they helped to get the monster up from a lying position. As befits its status as "king", *Tyrannosaurus rex* was among the most powerful of all dinosaur predators. It was also one of the last to become extinct.

**MONSTER MOUTH**
Holes found in the remains of *Tyrannosaurus's* victims tell us that its curved fangs punched deeply into flesh and bone. Pulling back, the monster tore out great mouthfuls of meat. Its jaw and neck were so strong that it could kill by shaking its victims apart.

Just as certain dinosaurs shared with birds features such as beaks and tail feathers, so mammals, too, seemed to be engaged in acts of shape-shifting. By the end of the Cretaceous period, placental mammals were emerging, so named because inside their mothers' bodies the developing babies are nourished by a special organ called a placenta. Early placental mammals included creatures very much like modern shrews, mice and rats, which spread rapidly over the Cretaceous world. Most were small, skulking creatures, venturing out only at night when the theropod dinosaurs slept.

**EARLY PLACENTAL**
The shrew-like Cretaceous mammal *Zalambdalestes* was a fast runner and jumped to escape predators. It fed on small arthropods.

There were also mammals known as marsupials, because the mothers nurture their young in a marsupium, a belly pouch. Marsupials once lived in many regions of the world, eventually becoming extinct as they were replaced by placental mammals. But the marsupials remained in Australia, after it had broken away from Antarctica and had become a single continent.

Here, in isolation from other competing species, the marsupials survived and prospered, giving rise to animals such as the koalas, possums, wallabies and kangaroos.

And what of the birds that had first flown in the skies of the Jurassic? They had multiplied beyond number in the Cretaceous period. One great group, known as the enantiornithines, included *Eoalulavis*, which was about the size of a sparrow. It had a tuft of feathers sprouting from its thumb to help it land and perch in trees. Another group included *Confuciusornis*, which had the claws and hips of the oldest birds but the toothless beak and short tail of later species. There were also birds that lost the ability to fly, such as the toothless seabird, *Hesperornis*.

**FEATHERED FLOCKS**
The crow-sized Cretaceous bird *Confuciusornis* perched in trees, ate plants and bred in colonies of hundreds. Males were distinguished by two long, showy tail feathers.

**HUNTER OR SCAVENGER?**
Some scientists argue that the heavy *Tyrannosaurus rex* was too slow to hunt live prey and instead scavenged from corpses killed by others.

This large species, which reached 2 m (6 ft) in length, resembled living diving birds and, like them, it swam for its prey. The flying birds were joined in the air by countless insects and by pterosaurs. Some had now grown so large that it is hard to imagine them getting off the ground.

**SOARING PTEROSAUR**
*Pteranodon's* colossal head crest may have acted as a "rudder" or stabilizer as it soared above the Cretaceous seas.

*Pteranodon* had a wingspan of some 9 m (30 ft), and an elaborate crest on the back of its head. It had a large jaw but no teeth, unlike Jurassic species such as *Pterodactylus*, which had dozens of teeth. Other flying reptiles were even larger, among them *Quetzalcoatlus*, which had the wingspan of a Second World War fighter plane.

The life under the Cretaceous seas was just as varied and perhaps more familiar. There were crabs and turtles as well as fishes resembling perch and herring. They shared the oceans with the extraordinarily long-necked plesiosaurs called elasmosaurs, and a new group of marine reptiles known as mosasaurs. Elasmosaurs were monstrous in size, and could grow to a length of 15 m (50 ft), while mosasaurs had terrifying jaws up to 1.5 m (5 ft) long. With their broad flippers and long tails, plesiosaurs and mosasaurs swam at great speeds in the Cretaceous seas.

**ANCIENT FLOWERS**
Today's beautiful magnolia first appeared during the mid-Cretaceous, which makes it one of the oldest flowering plants. Its defence against the ravages of herbivore dinosaurs was to grow rapidly.

Plants grew prolifically in the exceptional heat of the Cretaceous. With the emergence of the flowering plants, the landscapes became quite different from any of those in the previous ages. Their colourful arrival is as stupendous as the birth of flight or the emergence of the dinosaurs. The first flowers were weedy, soft-stemmed plants from which arose the ancestors of the birch and the palm, the oak and the lily, and the magnolia. The earliest known flowering plant is *Archaefructus* ("ancient fruit") believed to be at least 125 million years old. Cretaceous flowers developed petals and stamens like any modern from that period has been found preserved in amber. Insects such as bees and butterflies and wasps had evolved simultaneously with the flowering plants. It is as if a whole new environment, or ecosystem, had arrived in all its diversity and complexity, springing forth ready-made. This, of course, cannot be the case. There must have been a million false starts, breakdowns and failures. But the co-evolution of flowers and certain insects is still one of the most surprising of all the Earth's

developments. Yet much of the Earth's life was about to disappear. The Cretaceous was brought to an end by another huge extinction event, another prehistoric day of doom, in which 75 per cent of all the world's plant and animal species vanished. It destroyed the dinosaurs for ever. After a lifespan of some 165 million years they were wiped out by a cataclysmic event. The ammonites were also extinguished, having survived for more than 300 million years. The pterosaurs went. The mosasaurs went. Countless other marine animals also disappeared.

This terrible event, 65 million years ago, is known to scientists as the "K-T Boundary" (the K is for Kreide, meaning chalk in German; the T is for Tertiary, the next geological period). It is marked by a break

**LONG-NECKED GIANT**
Plesiosaurs such as *Elasmosaurus* "flew" gracefully through the water by flapping their two pairs of flippers alternately. Females may have heaved themselves ashore to lay eggs.

**BOUNDARY LAYER**
A dark line separating two layers of rocks in Italy is the evidence of a massive asteroid collision, which blew gas, dust and rock all over the world.

layers. The evidence of one form of life lies below it, and another kind of life above it. The world changed in the line marked by a centimetre or two of clay. Scientists have found something significant and unusual in this layer of clay – large amounts of a metallic element called iridium. Iridium is rare on the Earth, but much more commonly found in asteroids and meteorites. The element could, therefore, have come from an asteroid that smashed into the globe and destroyed much of the Earth's life. It was a chance event, but it changed the entire history of the planet. The scar left by the impact now lies hidden beneath rock and soil near the village of Chicxulub on the Mexican coast.

It is not easy to imagine the devastation such a collision would have caused. A few minutes after the impact, a whirlwind of fire would have blazed across the continent of America. The forests would have exploded, the rivers and lakes boiled. No plant or animal could have withstood the force and fury of the blast. A few hours later, giant waves would have swept across the whole world. Skies would have darkened as dust and smoke blotted out the Sun. Acid rain would have begun to

**DEEP IMPACT**
The asteroid that gouged out the Chicxulub crater in Mexico struck the Earth with a force 10,000 greater than all the world's nuclear bombs put together.

**CRATER IMPRESSION**
This artwork shows how the 180-km- (112-mile-) wide impact crater may have looked.

fall. Most dinosaurs in America would probably have died within a week. Any survivors would have been forced to wander across a blackened landscape, much like the one we imagine humans would face after a nuclear attack.

There are other theories to explain the extinction of the dinosaurs. For example, the end of the Cretaceous was a time of intense volcanic activity. These eruptions and explosions poured carbon dioxide into the atmosphere and the resulting haze obscured the Sun, causing plant life to wither and die. The fossil evidence also suggests that the dinosaurs had already been in decline for a long time because of falling temperatures as the tectonic plates carried certain regions nearer to the poles. As a result, there was a fall in numbers, and in diversity. All these forces seem to have worked together to produce the giant transition that is marked by the K-T Boundary, one of the most dramatic of all the catastrophes to affect the Earth.

There were winners, as well as losers, in the destruction at the end of the Cretaceous period. Certain groups of fern were not affected at all by the asteroid impact, or by climate change, which suggests that the Earth's plants are among the hardiest of all living things. More surprisingly perhaps, the birds survived. The fact that both mammals and birds are warm-blooded may help to explain their success. They were better equipped to cope with a cooling climate than large cold-blooded animals, which needed the Sun's heat to warm up. The decline of the large reptiles left more room for the mammals, which flourished in the following ages of the world to an extraordinary degree.

**END OF THE DINOSAURS**
The end-Cretaceous mass extinction was so severe that no land animal heavier than a large dog survived. Heavily built animals, such as this theropod, would have been among the earliest casualties.

**LIFE FROM THE ASHES**
The firestorms that followed the impact would have left a dead, charred world. Yet within a fairly short time, ferns became common as plants recolonized the devastated landscape.

END OF CRETACEOUS PERIOD

PALAEOCENE AND EOCENE EPOCHS | 65–34 MILLION YEARS AGO

# CHAPTER NINE

# A new *era* dawns

*The cataclysm that destroyed the dinosaurs also brought the curtain down on the **Mesozoic** era, "the age of middle life", which had lasted for 480 million years.*

THE NEW CENOZOIC ERA, in which we live today, began 65 million years ago. "Cenozoic" means "recent life", and in this time the modern world took shape. Great changes happened throughout the Cenozoic's first great period, the Tertiary. We now follow the Earth's history through the Tertiary's five epochs, as divisions of a geological period are called. These span more than 63 million years, beginning with the Palaeocene epoch, which lasted some ten million years. This may seem a brief spell compared with some of the massive lengths of time already described, but as we draw nearer to the modern age enough fossil evidence is available for us to peer in more detail at the prehistoric past and to separate the epochs more finely.

TERTIARY PERIOD                                    QUATERNARY PERIOD    TODAY

OLIGOCENE EPOCH    MIOCENE EPOCH    PLIOCENE EPOCH    PLEISTOCENE EPOCH    HOLOCENE EPOCH

In the Palaeocene epoch, the modern shape of the world was beginning
to assemble. Europe and North America had almost entirely drifted
apart, as the Atlantic Ocean continued to separate them. Portugal and
Spain were in the process of colliding with southern France, creating the
massive upflow of rock known as the Pyrenees. Italy was moving
northwards, helping to create the rippling in the Earth's crust called the
Alps. India was moving northwards, too, and when it finally drifted
against Asia the collision threw up the mighty range of mountains
known as the Himalayas. To see these mountains today is to understand
the gigantic forces that have shaped the continents of the world.

The Palaeocene world saw an evolutionary explosion of mammals.
Mammals had survived the extinction event that ended the Cretaceous
period, and, in the absence of any dominant reptile life, they spread

rapidly. Many were small creatures, living upon the floors of enormous forests, but within a fairly short space of time (about two or three million years) some had begun to grow much larger.

Mammal predators were in the making. One early group was especially vicious: the creodonts resembled a mixture between modern wolves, dogs and bears. Long, sharp front teeth for delivering a killer bite and slicing back teeth for crushing bone made them the chief meat-eating mammals of the Palaeocene. Their dominance did not save them from eventual extinction, however, unlike the other major meat-eaters of the epoch, the Carnivora – a group that eventually came to include modern cats and dogs. In fact, one early dog-like form did appear at this time – *Miacis* grew to about 30 cm (12 in) long. It might seem a cute, furry little beast, but it was a ferocious predator with claws that probably enabled it to scramble up trees to hunt its prey.

**JAWS OF A CREODONT**
This skull belonged to a vicious creodont known as *Hyaenodon*. Its jaw displays an array of strong fangs and crushing molar teeth.

Other predatory mammals had hoofs instead of claws. These were the mesonychians, and they too resembled wolves or bears, and some, hyenas. Unlikely as it seems, the early relatives of today's peaceful cows and sheep included these powerful, hoofed killers. From among the mesonychians, as we shall see, came the largest known carnivorous land mammal of all time.

**PRIMITIVE HOOFS**
*Phenacodus* was a sheep-sized Palaeocene herbivore with five toes on each foot, each ending in a small, blunt hoof. It belonged to a group of primitive hoofed mammals called condylarths.

**HORNS AND TUSKS**
Male *Uintatherium*
probably fought by
pushing each other
with their horns and
gouging one another
with their tusks.

Mesonychians sprang from among several groups of hoofed mammals
now appearing in the Palaeocene. The bulkiest, and strangest, were the
dinoceratans, or "terrible horns". These plant-eaters looked a little like
rhinoceroses, but had tusks and six knobbly horns on their heads. By
the next epoch, some had evolved to enormous sizes, among them
*Uintatherium*, which, although as large as an elephant, had a tiny brain.
Other hoofed animals resembled rats, sheep and horses. They lived
among the lush vegetation alongside a new and important group
of mammals fast appearing during the Palaeocene – the
primates. This group of animals was characterized by
having feet and hands that could grasp, large brains,
and forward-pointing eyes. Early types may have
looked like enormous squirrels. They had tails
and long fingers, and grew to
a length of almost 1 m (3 ft).
Others were closer to tree-
shrews in appearance, but from
these modest origins would emerge
monkeys, apes and finally humans.

The Palaeocene was also a testing
time for some weird "experimental"
mammal groups. A small, rodent-like
group known as multituberculates
were plant-eaters belonging to no
mammal group living today. Another
group, the taeniodonts, resembled
hybrids between squirrels and dogs, but with
great tusks, five-fingered clawed hands for rooting and

digging, and long, heavy tails. Some climbed trees in search of insects, eggs and leaves. By the mid-Eocene, the next epoch, they, too, were extinct and had left no living descendants.

The pterosaurs no longer flew after the end of the Cretaceous, but the birds survived and flourished. There were small birds, some similar to modern swifts, but perhaps the most surprising of the Palaeocene birds could not fly at all. These were the "terror birds", standing up to 2.5 m (8 ft) tall with monstrous, parrot-like beaks and powerful legs. One type was the mighty *Gastornis* (also known as *Diatryma*), a predatory carnivore that enjoyed unrivalled success and dominated the landscape for millions of years. It ran down its prey and killed them with its beak and claws – a truly terrifying bird. These large and voracious creatures were taking the place of the theropod dinosaurs at the top of the food chain. They adapted to the habitats of the dinosaur, and seemed to be replicating dinosaur behaviour. This is a remarkable aspect of evolution. Life seems to want to fill all available gaps, as if it hates to leave a "vacuum" in animal instincts and habits.

The terror birds survived through many of the epochs of the Tertiary period, a testimony to the success of certain evolutionary formulas. Nowhere is evidence for this clearer than among the fossils found in the Messel quarry, Germany. This quarry was the site of an ancient lake formed during the next epoch of the world, the Eocene. It has provided one of the most amazing images of prehistoric life yet discovered. Many of the creatures that thrived around the lake are familiar to us – their descendants still flourish today, 50 million years later.

The Eocene followed the Palaeocene and lasted from 55 to 34 million years ago. It is granted a separate name – from the Greek, meaning

**FEATHERED TERROR**
The monstrous "terror birds" lived in the Americas until about 400,000 years ago. Despite weighing up to 150 kg (330 lbs), they were agile predators, equipped with a powerful beak and three-toed feet capable of giving a savage, knockout kick.

"new dawn" – but in fact this epoch probably continued uninterrupted from the Palaeocene. We know this because in the Messel quarry palaeontologists have found 35 different species of mammal that were directly related to the mammal life of the previous epoch. There were bats and opossums, lemur-like primates and pangolins, as well as rats reaching a length of almost 1 m (3 ft). Most intriguingly, perhaps, are the remains of 70 primitive

horses called *Propalaeotherium* – animals that were much smaller than the ones we know today, reaching a height of only 60 cm (24 in) when fully grown. One of the most surprising aspects of prehistory is the difference of scale. The ancestors of cows and deer were also found within this site, but were only the size of rabbits.

From the fossilized remains of the Messel quarry it is possible for us to imagine the landscape around the ancient lake. There were palm trees and laurels, vines and citrus trees, as well as oaks and beeches. There were water lilies, as well as long weeds that drifted through the warm water. This primeval scene is one that may have looked strangely recognizable. It is a subtropical scene. Termites and ants, beetles and spiders flourished in the humid atmosphere. Frogs and toads, even tadpoles left fossilized remains. There were also turtles and crocodiles, and lizards that resembled modern iguanas, as well as a variety of snakes. However, there was one aspect missing from all Eocene snakes – they had no poison. These slithering creatures had yet to develop venom glands. The ancient lake was also teeming with

**SMALL SURVIVOR**
Small lizards thrived during the Eocene, but the number of reptile groups was by this time hugely reduced. Today, there are only three main reptile groups.

**FISH IMPRESSION**
Fine limestone has preserved some Messel lake bony fishes in remarkable detail.

bony fishes, including eels and ancestors of the perch, while in the oceans sharks were once more abundant.

The ancestors of modern whales had also arrived in this time span. Unlike sharks, whales are air-breathing mammals. The first were quite small, reaching a length of about 2 m (6 ft) and possessed limbs that allowed them to walk on land. Others were like ferocious seals and, like the seal, were adapted both to land and to sea. At a later point in the Eocene their limbs became shorter and less significant, as certain species adapted

**HIDDEN PERIL**
Danger may have lurked beneath the Messel lake in the form of poisonous volcanic gases. An eruption would have brought gas bubbling to the surface and killed the lake's inhabitants.

**EOCENE GIANT**
*Basilosaurus* is the
largest known fossil whale.
Its snake-like form was
more flexible than the
bodies of today's whales.

entirely to the sea. One of
them, *Basilosaurus*, matched the length
of large, modern whales but had a snake-like shape. It grew to a
length of 24 m (80 ft), and lived in shallow seas. *Basilosaurus* had
sharp teeth, and may have preyed on other mammals as well as fishes.

Life on land echoed that of life in the water, in the sense that a world
familiar to us now seemed to be dawning upon the continents. It is
heralded by the flying of bats, whose wings had evolved from the
outstretched hands of mammals that had once climbed the trees of
the forest. They kept their original mammals'
teeth, claws, and fearsome appearance, and indeed
have not fundamentally changed in 50 million years.

The more familiar and friendly cat and dog also represent
ancient forms. From a single shared ancestor that diversified
spectacularly, the cat and dog groups are part of the great
group of modern meat-eating mammals called the
Carnivora, which had first appeared in the Palaeocene. As
with most groups of animals, the cat group, or feliforms,
soon diverged into hundreds of different species large and
small. Eventually, some became hyenas, some became
mongooses; some became the famous sabre-toothed cats

**BAT GROUPS**
By the Eocene, bats had
split into today's two main
groups: insect-eating
microbats and fruit-eating
megabats. This fruit-eater
is known as a flying fox.

whose fossils are found in large numbers. Today's family pet is in turn
related to the prehistoric cat known as *Dinofelis*, or "terrible cat",
which grew to a length of 2.1 m (7 ft) and in its predatory habits was
similar to the modern leopard. The dog group, or caniforms, had also

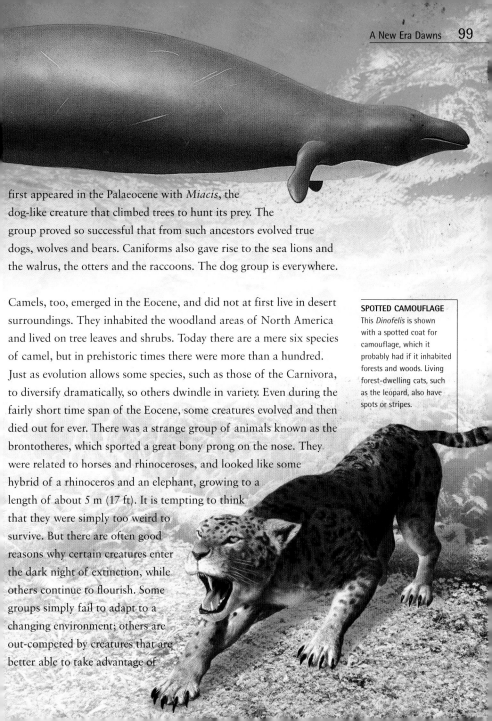

first appeared in the Palaeocene with *Miacis*, the
dog-like creature that climbed trees to hunt its prey. The
group proved so successful that from such ancestors evolved true
dogs, wolves and bears. Caniforms also gave rise to the sea lions and
the walrus, the otters and the raccoons. The dog group is everywhere.

Camels, too, emerged in the Eocene, and did not at first live in desert
surroundings. They inhabited the woodland areas of North America
and lived on tree leaves and shrubs. Today there are a mere six species
of camel, but in prehistoric times there were more than a hundred.
Just as evolution allows some species, such as those of the Carnivora,
to diversify dramatically, so others dwindle in variety. Even during the
fairly short time span of the Eocene, some creatures evolved and then
died out for ever. There was a strange group of animals known as the
brontotheres, which sported a great bony prong on the nose. They
were related to horses and rhinoceroses, and looked like some
hybrid of a rhinoceros and an elephant, growing to a
length of about 5 m (17 ft). It is tempting to think
that they were simply too weird to
survive. But there are often good
reasons why certain creatures enter
the dark night of extinction, while
others continue to flourish. Some
groups simply fail to adapt to a
changing environment; others are
out-competed by creatures that are
better able to take advantage of

**SPOTTED CAMOUFLAGE**
This *Dinofelis* is shown
with a spotted coat for
camouflage, which it
probably had if it inhabited
forests and woods. Living
forest-dwelling cats, such
as the leopard, also have
spots or stripes.

local conditions. The more recent extinctions of large mammals are due mainly, of course, to human hunting.

The Eocene also witnessed the arrival of groups whose evolutionary staying power has proved extraordinarily successful. The pig group appeared in this epoch and has survived for the last 40 million years. Some early species resembled the modern wild boar, while others looked like small buffaloes, but they were all defiantly swine-like. Over time, many species within the group evolved in shape or size according to their local environments. As a result, some became more aggressive, probably in order to fill a vacant niche for large carnivores. Some small forms of swine grew and grew in areas of North America, until one reached a length of 3.5 m (10 ft) and stood as tall as a man. This so-called "killer buffalo pig" lived on a diet of flesh and plants.

The elephants' ancestors and cousins also grew up in the Eocene. Or, rather, they became bulkier. The tiny creatures of the Palaeocene were just 60 cm (24 in) in height but were now replaced by larger and squatter animals. One of these Eocene proboscideans (the group that includes

**EVOLUTIONARY LUCK**
Evolution sometimes involves luck. For example, a cooling climate creates temperate regions, like this one, and may change vegetation in a way that favours some animals over others.

**FIGHTING FOR RIGHTS**
These *Brontops* belonged to a group of odd-toed, hoofed mammals called brontotheres. Skull injuries tell us that males fought each other with their horns, for dominance, territory or mating rights.

elephants and their extinct relatives) is known as *Moeritherium*. It resembled a long-bodied pig and had a primitive trunk like a protruding upper lip and nose. Proper trunks and tusks developed in other species so that, within 20 million years, the shape of the modern elephant can be seen in its ancestors. A later relative, known as *Arsinoitherium*, resembled a large rhinoceros with a mighty pair of horns on its face. It lived off the stems and leaves of plants.

One hoofed mammal of the Eocene that did not survive the passing of the millennia, however, is called *Andrewsarchus* ("Andrews' Flesh Eater") and it was the largest flesh-eating mammal ever seen on the globe. This mesonychian giant may have grown to a length of some 6 m (19 ft) and in appearance must have resembled a wolf from a fairy tale. Its massive jaws were powerful enough to kill other hoofed mammals with one bite, crushing their bones with huge back teeth.

As the great and ferocious animals died out, many smaller creatures lived on. These were better adapted for survival as the temperature of the Earth began to change once more. At the end of the Eocene epoch, the world grew cooler and less hospitable.

**SIMPLE GIANT**
The awkward-looking *Arsinoitherium* belonged to the same group of hoofed mammals as today's elephants. Its shoulders were powerfully muscled to support its huge weight, but its brain was small and simple.

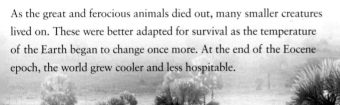

**ANDREWSARCHUS**
This monster is known only from its skull. Scientists have guessed its body shape.

# CHAPTER TEN

# Monkey
# business

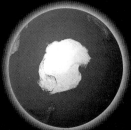

*The cooler epochs of the world
that followed the Eocene are
known as the* **Oligocene** *and
the* **Miocene**, *which between
them lasted some 29 million years.*

B Y NOW, THE WORLD MAP had finally settled into
its modern shape. Australia had moved into the zone
of the tropics, and Antarctica straddled the South
Pole, cut off from the other landmasses of the world. As
temperatures dropped, the Antarctic ice sheet began to
form. In this part of the Tertiary period Hawaii and Iceland
emerged from the seas as volcanic
islands. North and South America
remained cut off from each other;
the land bridge between them that
allowed the migration of animals
had not yet emerged from the sea.

Away from the equator, as climates cooled, the dense
tropical vegetation of the Eocene epoch gave way to
temperate and cold-climate forests, and wherever rainfall
became scarce, forests gave way to plains and prairies.

TERTIARY PERIOD

QUATERNARY PERIOD   TODAY

OLIGOCENE AND MIOCENE EPOCHS 34–5 MILLION YEARS AGO

**FAMILY OF GRASSES**
Today there are some 9,000 species of grass. Their inconspicuous flowers are pollinated by the wind.

These changes affected much of North America, Europe, Africa and Asia. South of a great northern belt of conifers, there were forests of oaks and maples interspersed by open glades. Between the trees a new plant grew: grass – that often overlooked and humble offspring of the Earth. It spreads both by seeds and by underground runners, and survives by growing new blades to replace those eaten by animals.

And so the prairies and savannahs and steppes emerged on the face of the Earth. These great plains

A herd of *Hipparion*

**THREE STOMACHS**
*Aepycamelus* had very long legs that enabled it to feed on tree leaves. It became extinct when the tree cover of its habitat disappeared. Like today's camels, it had three stomachs for digesting tough plant food.

of grass also allowed new forms of life to evolve. Again, we have an instance of evolution in action: a new environment giving rise to the types of animal that can best take advantage of that environment. In other words, as the grass arrived, so did mammals that evolved self-sharpening teeth, which could crop and chew up grass – a tough food full of hard silica. This process is called co-evolution. The grazers' droppings also fertilized the grass plants, so eaters and eaten both benefited. In nature, as we have already seen, everything connects.

So, with the spread of the grasslands, creatures began to move across them in the search for food. Many of these were animals with hoofs. They can be grouped according to whether their hoofs were even-toed

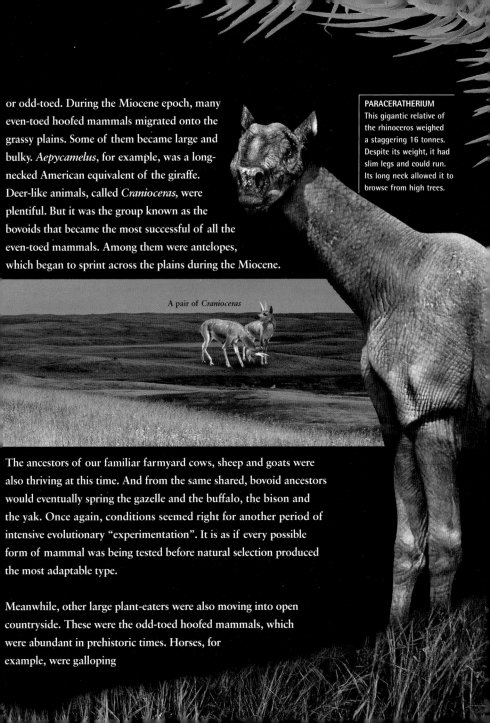

or odd-toed. During the Miocene epoch, many even-toed hoofed mammals migrated onto the grassy plains. Some of them became large and bulky. *Aepycamelus*, for example, was a long-necked American equivalent of the giraffe. Deer-like animals, called *Cranioceras*, were plentiful. But it was the group known as the bovoids that became the most successful of all the even-toed mammals. Among them were antelopes, which began to sprint across the plains during the Miocene.

**PARACERATHERIUM**
This gigantic relative of the rhinoceros weighed a staggering 16 tonnes. Despite its weight, it had slim legs and could run. Its long neck allowed it to browse from high trees.

A pair of *Cranioceras*

The ancestors of our familiar farmyard cows, sheep and goats were also thriving at this time. And from the same shared, bovoid ancestors would eventually spring the gazelle and the buffalo, the bison and the yak. Once again, conditions seemed right for another period of intensive evolutionary "experimentation". It is as if every possible form of mammal was being tested before natural selection produced the most adaptable type.

Meanwhile, other large plant-eaters were also moving into open countryside. These were the odd-toed hoofed mammals, which were abundant in prehistoric times. Horses, for example, were galloping

EVOLVING FOOT
Today's horses have one toe on each foot, but *Hipparion* had three. The central toe bore its weight.

EVOLVING FOOT
Today's horses have one toe on each foot, but *Hipparion* had three. The central toe bore its weight.

BURROWING RODENT
This rodent had huge claws and bizarre horns on its head, which may have helped with digging. Its small eyes suggest that it did not rely on sight too much.

GIANT DORMICE
The absence of large predators on the islands of Malta and Sicily meant that the dormouse *Leithia* could evolve to the size of a squirrel.

forwards in all shapes and sizes. They were no longer the small creatures that took shelter in woodland, eating soft-leaved plants. *Hipparion*, for instance, was some 1.5 m (5 ft) in length. It had teeth designed for chewing grass. And horses were joined by rhinoceroses, of which there were many species in the Oligocene and Miocene. Some were fast runners; some had short trunks. At a later date, one rhinoceros would grow a horn as long as 2 m (6 ft) on its forehead. Perhaps the most extraordinary specimen was the long-necked *Paraceratherium*, which has the distinction of being the largest land mammal ever to walk the Earth. It was 5.5 m (18 ft) high, and 9 m (30 ft) long, dwarfing the modern rhinoceros.

Yet it would be wrong for us to concentrate only on the larger mammals, because in the smaller forms there was a great burst of life and activity that has continued to the present day. There were beavers, for example, that made burrows in the shape of spirals. There were rabbits, hares and pikas looking very similar to their modern relatives. There was one extraordinary-looking horned rodent known as *Epigaulus*, which burrowed in the ground. The Miocene epoch has also given us plenty of evidence for the extraordinary phenomenon of separate evolutionary development. This occurs when environments cut off from the rest of the world produce some outlandish creatures. Certain islands in the

Mediterranean, for example, were isolated by high seas
for millions of years. In these habitats grew creatures
quite unlike anything in other areas
of the world. In Malta and Sicily
there was a giant dormouse that grew
to a length of 41 cm (16 in), which
might have come out of the pages of
*Alice in Wonderland*. On another island
there flourished giant hedgehogs, miniature
deer and giant owls – all of them developing
in strange ways because of their isolation
from the rest of the planet. When the first
people colonized the islands, these
creatures faded away, unable to
survive the competition from the
predatory animals that arrived with humans.

The most important group of mammals, however, has yet to be
described. They are significant because they herald our future life.
These were the primates, and they were changing. The earliest primates
had looked like squirrels or shrews, but in the early Tertiary period they
were replaced by two new groups that grew nails instead of claws.
They were the prosimians, or lower primates, such as the lemurs; and
the anthropoids, or higher primates, including monkeys, apes and,
eventually, humans. Anthropoids had bigger brains than prosimians.

By Miocene times, the anthropoid primates had split into two main
types. African and Asian apes and monkeys had forward-pointing
nostrils. The monkeys of South America had outward-pointing nostrils
and tails capable of gripping branches, as if with an extra
hand. It is not known how these South Americans
became separated from the rest. Perhaps their

**PLESIADAPIS**
The many primate groups
of the Oligocene and
Miocene may have
descended from primitive
forms of the Eocene epoch,
such as this *Plesiadapis*.
This animal resembled a
type of lemur, although
some scientists argue that
it was not a true primate.

**OUR APE ANCESTORS**
Humans are descended from the ancestors of African apes like these chimpanzees – tailless primates that swing below branches, arm over arm. Children swinging from climbing frames remind us of our ape ancestors.

ancestors floated across the Atlantic Ocean from Africa to South America on gigantic mats of vegetation. We have one major piece of evidence about the anthropoid primates of Africa and Asia – the "Old World" anthropoids. From the Miocene epoch, scientists have found the fossils of some that can be classified as hominoids. This is the group of anthropoid primates to which humans and apes belong. They had teeth and a limb structure similar to ours, and no tail. One type, called *Proconsul*, climbed trees in a fashion similar to a monkey. Another, an ape known as *Dryopithecus*, swung from branches, like a chimpanzee.

The fossil record shows that today's humans – upright-walking, large-brained primates – must have evolved from an ape-like, hominoid creature of the Miocene epoch. Many skulls of the in-between stages have been found, as well as some incomplete skeletons, although there is little evidence from the Miocene epoch itself. At some stage during that time, humans and apes shared a common ancestor. Unfortunately, there are few fossil-bearing rocks of this age in Africa, where these creatures evolved, so the tantalizing "missing link" – the creature that links our ancestors directly to the apes – has never been found. In fact, as we shall see, there are several missing links between modern humans and their distant ancestors and no clear lines of descent. The lineage is thoroughly muddled and uncertain.

**OLD WORLD ANCESTOR**
Living apes, such as gorillas, share an ancestor with the "Old World" monkeys of Africa and Asia, such as *Paracolobus*.

This uncertainty seemed only to increase in 2001, when scientists digging in the sand dunes of northern Chad, Africa, made a dramatic discovery. The Miocene skull they unearthed was about seven million years old. It seemed at first to be the skull of an ape, but on further examination its teeth appeared to be those of a hominid. Hominid, not to be confused with hominoid, is used here to mean the group to which only humans and their extinct ancestors the "ape-men" belong. The shape of the skull also suggests that it walked upright. But this creature was neither truly an ape nor on the evolutionary path that led to humans. It may have been an offshoot of the apes that died out, leaving no descendants.

Another possible hominid, some six million years old, was unearthed in Kenya. *Orrorin tugenensis*, as it is known, had teeth like a human's and seems to have walked upright. In some ways, it was more "human" than many of its successors. Indeed, there are a bewildering variety of possible human ancestors. We must remember that nothing is known for certain. The course of evolution is often wayward and unpredictable. There seem, in fact, to have been many different hominids, or hominid-like creatures, all living at the same time. Out of these the form called human eventually stepped forward.

**APE AND MONKEY**
*Proconsul* had the hands of a tree-climbing monkey, and the skull and shoulders of an ape. It lived in the forests of Miocene Kenya.

## DNA and evolution

In 1953, scientists discovered DNA – the chemical within cells that passes genetic information from one generation to the next. This provided a new way of studying evolution. For example, DNA evidence revealed that humans are more closely related to chimpanzees than to gorillas, and that during the Miocene humans and chimps shared a common ancestor before branching apart into two groups.

*A DNA molecule is like a ladder twisted into a spiral shape.*

### Genetic evidence
If two animals share a common ancestor, there will be similarities in the base pairs of their DNA. This can be used to verify the evolutionary trees worked out from fossils. DNA broadly confirms the theories of evolution.

*The rungs of the ladder are made of chemical compounds called bases. There are two per rung (called a base pair).*

END OF CRETACEOUS PERIOD

# CHAPTER ELEVEN

# Out *of* africa

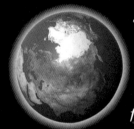

*The Tertiary period's final epoch was the **Pliocene**, which brings us to the threshold of the human. This epoch lasted from 5 to 1.8 million years ago.*

THE CONTINENTS HAD ASSUMED their modern form and location, but a generally humid climate was followed 2.8 million years ago by what is called the First Northern Glaciation. A north polar ice sheet had formed, and this transformed temperatures all over the world. It was a time in which the mammal life diversified even more.

There were now sloths as big as elephants and armadillos as long as limousines. *Smilodon*, the famous sabre-toothed cat, also emerged in the Pliocene. It grew to about 2.5 m (8 ft) in length, had retractable claws (claws that draw back into the paw), and a great jaw fitted with those 25-cm- (10-in-) long canine teeth that give it its name. Some of its prey may have included primates. During the Pliocene, certain ape-like creatures left the cover of the woodland and came to dwell upon the ground. This may not have been by deliberate choice. The drying of the climate may have led to the destruction of the forests, so that the apes were forced to live in open countryside. Over many millennia, they learned to stand and to walk upright, itself a momentous advance in the history of the world. This revolutionary adaptation may have helped to protect them, because by standing upright they could see much further over grasses and rocks.

More importantly, however, is the fact that the hands of these creatures were now free to perform other functions. This single development heralds the progress of humankind itself. It represents the birth of the possibility of technology. Hands that had previously foraged for food upon the ground could now, over time, make axes and spears.

In the 1990s, scientists found skeletons in Ethiopia dated at between 4.4 and 5 million years old. They belonged to *Ardipithecus ramidus*, a name meaning "ground-ape-root". Popularly known as

**SABRE-TOOTHED BITE**
*Smilodon* used its enormous specialized teeth to deliver a suffocating bite to the neck or to sever its prey's spinal cord. It probably hunted in packs.

"ape-men", somewhat similar creatures had long been the subject of films and comic books. The real evidence, however, is far more interesting than any fictional account. The skull shape of Ethiopian *ramidus* means that it walked on two legs, and was a hominid of about 1.2 m (4 ft) in height. But it also had ape-like features, such as large canine teeth and long arms. Some scientists believe that it walked and hunted for food on the ground, but slept in the trees that dotted the plains. Others argue that *ramidus* was a woodland creature entirely, thus overturning the theory that hominids walked upright as a means of moving across the African plains.

In short, it is a puzzle. It suggests the mixed and muddled nature of human origin. There is no simple evolutionary ladder, with various steps leading to and from the "missing link". If we were to draw a diagram of the evolutionary paths of our ancestors, it would look rather like a complex bush of life with branches leading in many directions. Some early creatures, for example, had more human characteristics than later ones. Like the creature found in northern Chad, *ramidus* itself may have been neither hominid nor ape but something in between. The species anyway became extinct – yet another hominid prototype that lost the struggle of life.

We learned a great deal about early hominid life after scientists in Kenya discovered pieces of a skeleton with an age of 4.2 million years. This was an australopithecine ("southern ape"), the name given to our earliest ancestors after the evolutionary split between apes and humans.

**PLANET OF THE APES**
Popular stories of "ape-men" derive from the monkey-like shape of some early hominid skulls. In fact, these creatures' muzzles were generally shorter than those of apes and they had arc-shaped rows of teeth, like a human's, as this model of an australopithecine skull shows.

## Evidence of upright walking

Two key features separate hominids from other apes: large brains and upright walking (bipedalism). Footprints found at Laetoli, in Tanzania, have been dated at 3.75 million years old. They show the imprint of an arch and a big toe closer to a human's than an ape's (see comparison below). This tells us that free-striding, upright walking had evolved by that date.

**Gorilla foot**
A gorilla has curved toes and an inwardly twisting big toe adapted more for grasping, like a human hand, than for walking.

**Human foot**
The human foot and toes have become long and flat for easy walking and balancing. The big toe is aligned with the others.

**Footprints in the ash**
The Laetoli footprints are preserved in hardened volcanic ash. They were made by *Australopithecus afarensis*, the only hominid known to have existed in this part of Africa at the time.

The jaw of this creature appeared part human and part ape. It stood upright and probably lived in a woodland habitat along with the forest monkeys whose remains were found around it. This creature became known as *Australopithecus anamensis*, meaning "southern ape of the lake". It will not be the last creature, however, that scientists will discover and name. There may still be many species to be unearthed, further complicating the record. It is no accident that all of these early hominid forms have been discovered in Africa. All the evidence suggests that this continent was indeed where human life began.

In Ethiopia, excavators had already found the remains of another early species of australopithecine. *Australopithecus afarensis* died out three million years ago after possibly surviving for a million years. It walked upright, but we know from its finger bones that it may have climbed trees. Its limbs were human in shape, and the height of the male was some 1.5 m (5 ft). The male also had a crest upon the top of its skull, and both sexes shared prominent brow ridges, and faces that projected forwards, like those of chimpanzees.

This creature would not have looked very "human" – its jaw was that of an ape. However, its toes resembled human toes. And there is evidence to support this. In 1976,

scientists in Laetoli, Tanzania, made a dramatic discovery. Two sets of almost-human footprints, with the imprint of toe and heel, had been fossilized in volcanic dust. The scientists must have been as amazed, and as awe-struck, as Robinson Crusoe finding the footprints on the sand of his desert island. But theirs was by far the more important find.

**ROBUST PLANT-EATERS**
Some australopithecines had heavily built skulls and massive jaws, probably used for eating tough grain rather than meat.

These creatures walked like humans, too. From the footprints they left we can see that they carried their weight in a similar way. The two had walked closely together, but one had hesitated for a moment before going forward. Maybe they walked side by side; one may even have put its arm around the other's shoulder. They were walking on an African plain, a savannah, with pockets of acacia trees around them; a volcano, called Sadiman, was smoking in the distance. Its dust covered the ground on which they walked. So we may picture these primeval *afarensis* hominids keeping company with one other in a dangerous environment.

**AUSTRALOPITHECINES**
Hominids may have started walking upright because of a changing environment. As forest gave way to savannah, they may have needed to move across open spaces quickly and efficiently, using long strides. Free hands would have allowed them to carry food, children and weapons.

Back in Ethiopia, perhaps the most famous *afarensis* find was the skeleton known as "Lucy" (if it is indeed female), discovered buried in a ravine. From her remains we can see that she was less than 1.2 m (4 ft) tall and had suffered from arthritis. In the same region, palaeontologists found evidence of 13 other *afarensis* grouped together. All had been killed suddenly by some natural catastrophe about

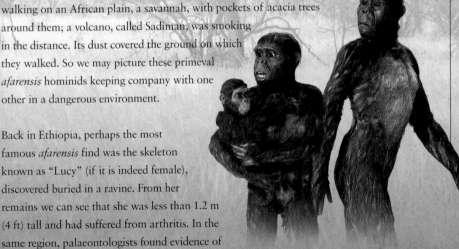

**LUCY'S BONES**
The most complete *afarensis* skeleton found was nicknamed Lucy. This model shows how she may have looked.

3.2 million years ago, perhaps drowned by a flash flood. They had died together, which suggests that they formed a community, possibly for protection. In a habitat that included sabre-toothed cats, there would have been safety in numbers.

The *afarensis* males were much larger than the females, suggesting that, like gorillas, they competed aggressively with each other for mates. But there is also the evidence of the two creatures walking closely together in Laetoli – which implies, possibly, that male and female strolled side by side as equals. Perhaps these creatures were at some halfway state of existence – neither fully ape nor fully human. There is one other interesting fact about the discoveries in Africa. No evidence of stone tools of any kind was found with the skeletons. Their brains had not developed enough for the next leap to be made. That would come, as we shall see, from a surprising quarter.

In the same epoch, there lived in Africa another hominid so different from *Australopithecus afarensis* that scientists have placed it in a separate genus, or biological group. *Kenyanthropus platyops* had a flattened face and small teeth, more similar to some later species than to any other creature of the time. The discovery has raised more questions than answers, and so only adds to the mystery of human origins.

Yet certain discoveries have been made that do help clarify the long history of hominids. In South Africa, the first-ever fossil-find of an australopithecine was the skull of a young child in which the teeth were close to being human. The creature was promptly called *Australopithecus africanus*, and is seen as another example of early hominid diversity. Interestingly, the child's skull was found with the bones of other mammals and all had been scraped by an eagle's beak. Some large bird must have

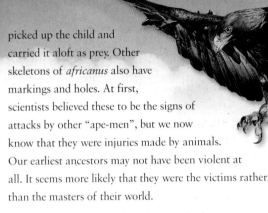

picked up the child and carried it aloft as prey. Other skeletons of *africanus* also have markings and holes. At first, scientists believed these to be the signs of attacks by other "ape-men", but we now know that they were injuries made by animals. Our earliest ancestors may not have been violent at all. It seems more likely that they were the victims rather than the masters of their world.

This leads to one of the most extraordinary discoveries in the history of hominid life. In 1996, scientists found some 2.5-million-year-old fossils in Ethiopia that they named *Australopithecus garhi* (in that country garhi means "surprise"). This hominid had long legs like a human's but, much more importantly, the world's oldest stone tools were found close to the site, which raises the possibility that this species was a remote ancestor of modern humans. The tools had been used to scrape meat from antelopes' bones and to extract the juicy marrow from inside. *Australopithecus garhi* may have been a scavenger (one that feeds on the remains of prey killed by carnivores). It co-existed with other species of hominid, among them *Australopithecus aethiopicus*. This was a heavily built creature with a flat face, no forehead and a ridge upon its skull. Its teeth suggest that it was a herbivore, and therefore quite different from the meat-eating *garhi*. It appears that several very different species of hominids were living on the same continent at the same time.

Such hominids also shared their world with a creature called *Homo habilis*. Its name means "handy man" or "well-adapted man", because of the tools found with its remains. It is the oldest species to be granted the name of "homo" ("man") because it was thought to be the distant ancestor of *Homo sapiens*. Its crudely chipped stone tools, nearly two

**HOMINID SENSATION**
When palaeontologist Raymond Dart found this *Australopithecus africanus* skull in 1924, he caused a sensation by describing it as an early hominid. The other experts of the time were convinced that this was the skull of an ape. It was some 20 years before later findings confirmed that Dart was right.

**DINNER TOOL**
This pebble tool, found in the Olduvai Gorge in Tanzania, was probably used by *Homo habilis* to smash open bones or hard fruit.

million years old, could have been used to scrape off meat or extract bone marrow, but they could also have been used for pounding fruit and seeds. *Homo habilis* was an omnivore, an eater of many types of food, and its varied diet may have allowed it to travel for longer distances than the more ape-like creatures of its time, which relied upon more local sources of food. Its brain was much larger than the australopithecines, and more human in shape. Its mobility and larger brain may also have meant that it could better cope with the effects of climate change.

Its similarity to *Homo sapiens*, however, turned out to be deceptive. *Homo habilis* still possessed long ape-like arms – longer than those of the earlier *afarensis* known as Lucy – and the creature was still small, only 1.0–1.5 m (3–5 ft) tall. Also, the fact that the simple technology of *habilis*'s tools shows no signs of development suggests that its brain made no great evolutionary progress.

**PREHISTORIC DIET**
*Homo habilis*'s diet would have included seeds, fruit, shoots, leaves, meat and bone marrow. Most environments would have yielded something that *habilis* could eat.

However, about 1.9 million years ago, there emerged the first undoubted member of our genus, Homo. *Homo ergaster*, or "work man", was a tall creature with a large brain, low skull, brow ridges and protruding jaws. The most complete specimen comes from Kenya. It was a boy of about 11 years, who was already 1.7 m (5 ft 6 in) tall, with long legs and narrow hips. He had died in swampland some 1.5 million years ago. If he had lived he would have grown taller than 1.8 m (6 ft). The shape and size of his limbs meant that he was a good runner across the scorching plains and lived in an extremely hot climate. A tall slender body shape maximizes the surface area of the skin, helping to cool the body quickly in hot climates through sweating.

**FLAT FACE**
Once thought to belong to *Homo habilis*, this rather flat-faced skull belonged to a more human-like species known as *Kenyanthropus*.

His body was probably covered in fine, short hair and, to minimize the effects of the solar rays, his skin was no doubt dark. So we see rising before us a creature surprisingly close to ourselves. With its smooth skin and its long legs, its height and its ability as a hunter or as a scavenger, *Homo ergaster* could have been mistaken for a naked human.

It would have appeared much more human than another ape-like animal that flourished at the same time, between one and two million years ago. *Paranthropus robustus* ("robust near-man") was found in South Africa. This close relative of the australopithecines lived on plants and shoots. Although small and small-brained, this beast was powerfully built, as its name suggests. Yet it may have used tools, also, and so spoils any carefully drawn picture of one group evolving from another group with unique skills. What we have instead is a complicated picture of different hominids making their separate ways through the African world.

**APE FEATURES**
Despite its large brain size, which enabled it to make simple tools, recent discoveries show that *Homo habilis*'s body had ape-like proportions. *Habilis* may in fact have been a species of australopithecine, and not part of our genus, Homo.

We are on clearer ground, however, with the species known as *Homo erectus*. But few things in prehistory are ever simple or uncontroversial. Some scientists think *Homo erectus* was an advanced Asian offshoot of Africa's *Homo ergaster*, while others think both belonged to the species *Homo erectus*. If both were separate, *erectus*'s first appearance has been dated at about 1.8 or 1.7 million years ago. It was close in size to the modern human, and its brain capacity was more than two-thirds of our own. Interestingly, in the long and slow course of its existence upon the Earth the brain of *Homo erectus* grew larger.

## Brain size

The size of the brain, an indicator of intelligence, is one factor in explaining why some species survive while others die out. Over the course of hominid evolution, the brain has tripled in size. Early hominid brains were little bigger than those of gorillas, but in terms of brain to body ratio, they were midway between apes and humans.

**Australopithecine brain**
The brain of a robust australopithecine, one of the larger species, was 500 cc.

**The modern human brain**
Today's humans have brains of about 1,400 cc. The brain to body ratio is high, and the forebrain, the seat of reason, is large.

There is a biological fact connected with the increase of brain size. As hominids evolved bigger brains, their babies were born proportionately less developed, with most brain growth taking place after birth. This is because a big-brained baby could not have passed through its mother's birth canal. It is possible, therefore, that a newborn *Homo erectus* was utterly helpless and would have needed much care and protection in order to survive. It might have been born into a world where there was already some sense of human longing and belonging.

There is another biological tendency to be seen in the fossils of these long-dead hominids. The australopithecine males were much taller than the females. In early Homo species, on the other hand, the male and female were similar in height. This suggests equality of another kind, too: scientists now accept that the male and female members of the group entered into life-long relationships and did not engage in herd-like sexual behaviour. In other words, the males probably did not compete with each other for a mate.

Both forms of early Homo proved successful and enduring. *Homo ergaster* was the first to move out of Africa. Within a few thousand years it had reached Asia and the edge of Europe. *Homo erectus* had travelled as far as Indonesia by

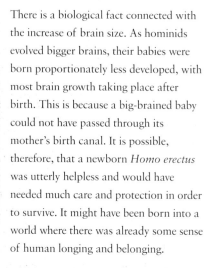

**HUNTER-SCAVENGER**
*Homo ergaster* probably both hunted prey and scavenged from carcasses, which it butchered with stone tools.

1.8 million years ago. For nearly two million years it thrived in the warmer parts of Asia. The genus Homo might have wandered as soon as it emerged into the world; its historic destiny, as it were, to populate the planet. Whatever drove migration, we know that *ergaster* and *erectus* adapted well to a range of environments. This was partly because they were omnivores. Their varied diet meant that they could survive in difficult conditions. Meat and fat were also a source of energy and, in time, a means of increasing the power and complexity of the brain.

A more developed brain was probably the reason why *ergaster* and *erectus* were capable of creative activity. Their tools have different features in different parts of the world, unlike those of the earlier *Homo habilis*, which showed no alteration in a million years. By 1.6 million years ago, chipped-stone hand axes and cleavers had appeared in Africa. These tools, belonging to *ergaster*, were for butchering large carcasses, suggesting that it had perhaps become a big-game hunter and not just a scavenger of big cats' kills.

Hunting and meat-eating raises an interesting question. Had early Homo learned the secret of fire? From the evidence of heat fractures on stone tools some believe that humans may have discovered fire about 1.6 million years ago. And did they speak? Again, no one knows. That extraordinary transformation, without which humankind could not have emerged, is shrouded in darkness. The evidence of the only good fossilized skeletons is unclear. Nerve channels in the chest vertebrae may have been too narrow to allow the easy control of breathing needed for clear speech. But nothing is agreed. And were they, after all, "human"? If you had greeted one, would there have been some stir of recognition in its eyes? Would it have greeted you in return, knowing that the two of you were in some fundamental way alike? It is an unanswerable question.

**COHABITATION**
Different diets and habitats may be the reason why several species of hominid co-existed in Africa without conflict.

**HOMO ERECTUS SKULL**
*Homo erectus* had a brain size close to that of today's humans, about 1,100 cc.

END OF CRETACEOUS PERIOD

# CHAPTER TWELVE

# Of ice *and* men

*The migration of early humans brings us into the present period, the* **Quaternary***. Its first epoch, the* **Pleistocene***, saw the rise of* Homo sapiens *("wise man").*

THE PLEISTOCENE BEGAN 1.8 million years ago with a general cooling of the world and the formation of vast, thick ice sheets in the northern regions of Asia, Europe and America. The cold lasted for 90,000 years, followed by a warm period of about 10,000 years. There have been 20 such glacial phases, so that the climate has been in a state of slow but continuous change up to the present day. We are today living in a warm (interglacial) phase of a great ice age. As ice sheets shrank and expanded, the level of the seas rose and fell, lands were submerged and then exposed again, plains turned into lakes, which became ice, and seafloors were exposed and became covered in forest or tundra (treeless, Arctic plains). A land ridge across the Bering

Strait linked Asia and North America, thus allowing the free passage of species across the continents. North America and South America were by now joined by the Isthmus of Panama. These climatic changes had a number of different causes, the most important being continental drift and the alarming reality of the Earth orbiting further away from the Sun, which affected the amount of heat reaching the surface. The last glaciation of the present ice age ended about 10,000 years ago. It would seem on past experience that a cold phase is about to begin, but, of course, global warming caused by human activity may mean that it is indefinitely postponed.

**WOOLLY MAMMOTH**
Mammoths moved in great herds across the Pleistocene grasslands, feeding on small plants, which they plucked with two "fingers" on the tips of their trunks. Their tusks were used for combat and for display, and as tools for gathering food.

At the beginning of the Pleistocene, there were mammals in abundance. In the warmer regions there grew giant sloths taller than any elephant, some 7 m (20 ft) in height when they reared up, and armadillos about 3 m (10 ft) long. These creatures, with their rigid shells of bony plates, resembled tanks. But of course there were also the cold weather beasts that had evolved to survive the icy climate, among them reindeer, elk, giant deer, polar bears and a species of rhinoceros that had grown a woolly coat in order to protect itself from the bitter cold.

Perhaps the best known of the glacial creatures is the woolly mammoth. It was essentially an elephant covered with fur. But its domed skull, its curved tusks and its shoulder hump have made it instantly recognizable as the lost creature of the ice age. Many specimens have been found, buried virtually intact in the permafrost (subsoil that remains frozen all year). Woolly mammoths grew to a height of about 3.5 m (11 ft), and foraged on the ice age grasslands. They were survivors, too, and lasted for more than a million years. The last were believed to have lived as recently as 4,000 years ago on an Arctic island off Siberia. They feature in cave paintings, dated about 30,000 years ago, where some are pictured fighting or moving in herds.

In the warmer interglacial periods, elephants and various species of horse and cattle thrived. There were antelopes and bison, sheep and goats, all roaming wild across the landscape. There were various species of the cat group, among them the hyenas and the sabre-toothed *Smilodon*. The wolves flourished, among them *Canis dirus*, or "fearful hound". One creature, known as

**MASSIVE MEGATHERIUM**
This Pleistocene sloth grew to the size of an elephant. Today's sloths are no larger than medium-sized dogs.

**GOLDEN FIND**
This baby mammoth lay frozen for 40,000 years until discovered intact by gold miners in Russia, in 1977.

**BIG JAW**

The jawbone of *Homo heidelbergensis* combined primitive and modern features. Its shape was large and thick, but the molar teeth were as small as those of *Homo sapiens*.

**ANCESTRAL OX**

*Bos primigenius* was the ancestor of today's domesticated cattle. Unlike modern cattle, however, this Pleistocene giant was wild and aggressive.

*Bos primigenius*, or "ancestral ox", grew to a height of more than 2 m (6 ft), was 3 m (10 ft) in length, and grew large, spreading horns. Yet here is an astonishing fact – the last member of this species was killed in Poland in 1627. It had survived the dawning of the modern world. In the seas of the Pleistocene there flourished other "modern" creatures such as seals and sea lions. There were also diving birds called great auks, which were not finally killed off by humans until 1844. There were pine trees and grapevines, oaks and spruces and buttercups. And, finally, there were humans.

At this stage in prehistory there was a fairly rapid development of human abilities. About 700,000 years ago, while *Homo erectus* was still making its way through the forests and streams of Africa and Asia, an altogether more intelligent creature had emerged. This was *Homo heidelbergensis*, a tall, tough creature named after the city in Germany where its jaw was first discovered. Its remains have since been found as far apart as England and Zambia.

We know that *heidelbergensis* had skills from the remains of its tools, among them spears and hammers. The evidence of hand axes, cleavers and bones shows that these early hunters formed groups before carefully choosing and stalking their prey. They then butchered the carcasses in a methodical manner, suggesting some kind of intelligent, communal activity. *Homo heidelbergensis* no doubt used fire to cook its meat. It may also have worn clothing, and even built huts. But the larger question concerns its use of speech, that breath of power that would eventually control the world. A group that had skills for hunting and cooking must have evolved some system of communication, but the use of language can neither be proved nor disproved.

We may enter the mind of *heidelbergensis* in another way, however, because we know that it deliberately disposed of its dead. A cave complex in northern Spain, called the "Pit of Bones", contains the remains of many human skeletons. They are about 300,000 years old. Their large noses show that they had adapted to the colder conditions of Pleistocene Europe. A bigger nose allowed them to warm the freezing air before it entered their lungs. Why bodies were brought to the Pit of Bones is a mystery. Did *heidelbergensis* have some notion of an afterlife, which led it to make such an enclave for the dead?

If we look at what came after *heidelbergensis*, there may be the glimmerings of an answer. There was a group of hominid creatures that buried their dead in graves, apparently leaving offerings with the body or sprinkling the corpse with coloured powders. They were the ritual tokens of *Homo neanderthalensis*, a group that, over many thousands of years, may have evolved from *Homo heidelbergensis*. *Homo neanderthalensis*, better known as the Neanderthals,

## Toolmaking

Crafting a tool involves using memory, planning ahead and working out abstract problems. Learning to make tools marked the beginning of humans' use of technology to help them adapt to their environment.

Pebble hammer

Bone hammer

**Flintworking**
In Stone Age Europe, flint was the most suitable material for toolmaking. When carefully chipped, rough flint may be crafted into a variety of shapes and sizes. Like glass, flint can be sharpened into a fine cutting edge.

Regular flakes are chipped off with a stone hammer.

The flint is trimmed with a bone hammer.

**Hand axe**
This chipped-stone axe, found in Swanscombe, England, fitted into the palm of the hand.

**BONE CRUNCHER**
*Canis dirus* had stronger jaws and bigger teeth than today's wolves, and so was better at breaking and eating bones.

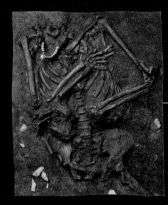

**RITUAL BURIAL**
This Neanderthal body has been laid on its back with its arms over its chest.

were much shorter and stockier than their predecessors – about 1.70 m (5 ft 6 in) in height as compared to 1.80 m (6 ft) – probably because their bodies needed to conserve warmth in a cold climate. They represent another evolutionary line of adaptation and change. The Neanderthals emerged some 250,000 years ago, and spread all over Europe and parts of the Middle East. They had broad noses and a characteristic bump at the back of the skull. They possessed ridges along their brows,

**NEANDERTHAL LOOK**
Neanderthals may have been light-skinned. They were probably the first people to wear clothes.

and sloping foreheads. Their somewhat formidable appearance has given them a reputation as a primitive or backward race, with the word "neanderthal" used as a term of abuse.

In fact, Neanderthals had a larger brain capacity than today's humans, varying from 1,200 cc to 1,750 cc as opposed to the range of 1,200 cc to 1,600 cc in *Homo sapiens*. This does not necessarily mean that they were more intelligent, but it does imply that they were just as responsive and as sensitive to their surroundings. They had certainly mastered the art of making fire, and hearths have been found on the floors of caves. It is not difficult for us to imagine a clan gathering around the hearth, perhaps talking to each other. Their skeletons suggest that they were capable of speech, but we can only guess at what its quality and sound were like.

The tools of the Neanderthals were more advanced than those of *heidelbergensis*. Sharp blades fitted neatly into wooden implements. Neanderthal sites have also yielded simple necklaces made from the teeth of animals – personal ornaments that were perhaps worn as status symbols. There is evidence that communities cared for their old and sick. But before the picture of Neanderthal life becomes too rosy, we should note that they may also have been cannibals. Theirs was a hard life; most of the injuries they sustained were the result of clashes with large animals. The climate was at times very cold, and their lives generally short. They lived for about 220,000 years in these harsh conditions and developed a fairly sophisticated culture. Yet, about 30,000 years ago, they disappeared from the Earth record. They became extinct.

The Neanderthals represent a dead end that could not reach towards full humanity. Recent DNA evidence supports this conclusion, with

**THICK HEAD**
The Neanderthal skull has a low, flat crown, a receding chin and a very prominent brow ridge. Powerful neck muscles attached to the swelling at the back.

*Neanderthals made a wide variety of stone tools and weapons. This flint scraper was used to prepare skins.*

**WOOD WORK**
Neanderthals used wooden throwing spears when hunting. These were sharpened to a point and hardened with fire.

## The making of fire

Fire was the greatest discovery made by prehistoric people. It enabled them to keep warm when the climate became much colder than it is today, it helped them to keep wild animals at bay and hardened the tips of wooden spears. Fire also cooked food, making certain indigestible meats and plants edible, and so enlarged the food supply. The great advance came when people found out how to make fire by rubbing sticks together to create heat.

**Fire drill**
This simple fire drill (right) was rotated in the palms of both hands to generate heat on the wood underneath. Dry straw ignited by the heat would be added to a heap of small sticks, surrounded by stones (left).

*Stones protected fire from draughts.*

*Wooden drill*

*Holes where drill has been used.*

signs of important differences in the DNA of *Homo sapiens* and Neanderthal groups. Although they were similar to us in many ways, there is an unmistakable difference. The Neanderthals were "like" humans, but they lacked the insights that make us unique.

**STRONG AND SLIM**
Cro-Magnons were a European group of *Homo sapiens*. They were muscular and well built but lacked the thick bones of Neanderthals. They protected their bodies with clothes made of furs and skins.

Most palaeontologists agree that *Homo sapiens* emerged out of Africa, perhaps evolving from a form of *Homo heidelbergensis*. He and She first appeared about 180,000 years ago. They were tall, and probably lived on grasslands or coastlines where food could be most easily gathered. The size and shape of the head were human. The bone structure was lighter than that of previous hominids, and indeed seems to be growing lighter all the time. The teeth and jaws were shrinking to human size, as were arms, hands and feet.

The structure of *Homo sapiens* allowed for flexibility and adaptability in a variety of habitats. And, indeed, groups of *Homo sapiens* began to spread, reaching Australia via Indonesia by 60,000 years ago. They arrived in Europe some 40,000 years ago (10,000 years before the disappearance of Neanderthals on that continent). This extraordinary and rapid colonization of the planet is an indication of *Homo sapiens'* success in every sphere of life. Ours is indeed the most successful group of mammals ever to emerge, and has in the course of its brief evolution transformed the Earth on which it appeared less than 200,000 years before. We must remember that, in the context of the Earth's long history, these are minuscule sections of time. The time span for the whole evolution of humankind is no more than a pinprick at the apex of the Great Pyramid, a lick of paint on the top girder of the Eiffel Tower.

Europe's first fully modern humans are known as Cro-Magnons, named after a site in France where they were first found. They arrived on the continent some 40,000 years ago as direct descendants of the original *Homo sapiens*. Scattered among their bones, archaeologists have found a range of sophisticated tools and weapons, including harpoons and needles as well as knives and spear-points. They built dwellings – some using the bones of mammoths – and they stitched clothing from the furs and skins of animals. They also wore jewellery; necklaces of shells and teeth have been found.

For the first time in the history of the planet there now lived people who created art. Figurines, carved out of stone or

**TODAY'S SKULL**
The human skull differs significantly from the Neanderthal by having a flat, prominent forehead, a smaller nose, and smaller teeth. This makes the face fairly straight and flat rather than forward-jutting.

**HUMAN MIGRATION**
*Homo sapiens* spread rapidly across the world through Asia, reaching North and South America via land bridges. In time, people also built sailing boats to reach remote Pacific islands.

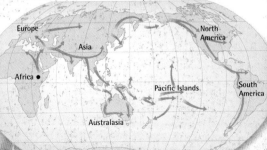

Europe

Asia

North America

Africa ●

Pacific Islands

South America

Australasia

**SOCIETY BURIAL**
Important Cro-Magnons like this one were buried with ornaments and the trappings of social rank.

ivory, have been unearthed all over Europe, some as delicate as anything out of Greece or Rome. In a Russian grave three bodies were found covered with thousands of ivory beads. These were clearly important people, which suggests that the world of the Cro-Magnons already had a hierarchy of authority.

But our clearest view of the Cro-Magnons and their kin outside Europe are surely through cave paintings. There are outline drawings of bison and panthers, of mammoths and rhinoceroses, of cattle and antelopes. There are outlines of human figures, too, together with the handprints of these ancient painters. Their skilful and intense pictures of the world are painted in profusion, and are full of energy and motion. That these people were skilful artists is not in doubt, although we still do not understand the role of their work. Possibly the paintings were connected with rituals that took place in the caves, or may even be representations of the artists' dreams. Whatever the explanation, it has long been shrouded in silence and mystery.

**ART AND CRAFT**
*Homo sapiens* is unique in producing art and fine, crafted tools. These were often decorated, and designed for delicate work. Seen here are carved figurines, an ivory knife for cutting snow and a finely crafted harpoon head.

*Cave artists used small bones to paint with ochre and charcoal.*

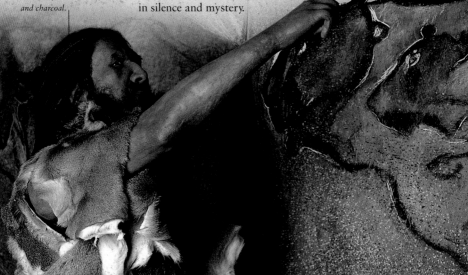

About 30,000 years ago, *Homo sapiens* was alone upon the Earth. All other hominid groups had become extinct, leaving the closest relations to humans among the chimpanzees and gorillas, which had started on their own separate paths.

The start of the last cold phase of the present ice age can also be dated to about 30,000 years ago. It lasted for some 17,000 years. When the ice finally retreated, our own era began. It is known as the Holocene, or Recent epoch. *Homo sapiens* had by now colonized most of the regions of the Earth, but with mixed consequences. Many animals of the cold Pleistocene epoch silently disappeared, their extinction largely brought about by human hunting. In the first three or four thousand years after the last cold phase ended, various groups of *Homo sapiens* discovered the advantages of farming – of sowing crops and of breeding animals. But that is part of another story. It is the story of human civilization. This story must end with the final emergence of *Homo sapiens* as the dominant species upon the planet. Its reign has not yet been long, and may have incalculable consequences for the Earth, but we have learned that humankind can trace its origins to that first fiery moment when the Universe began. Fire is the central point, as it was in the beginning, as it still is at the centre of our world. Even today, when we gather around a fire at night, we may be driven by very ancient forces indeed.

**ANCIENT FIRE**
South African Xhosa boys are seated around a fire for an initiation ritual that has changed little since the days of their ancient ancestors.

# Fossils

FOSSILS ARE THE REMAINS of ancient animal and plant life that have been preserved naturally for millions of years. They range from the bones of the largest dinosaurs to the tiniest bacteria. A fossil may show the structure of an organism in amazing detail. Leaves, flowers, feathers, teeth, even footprints can all be fossilized. Special conditions are needed for fossilization to occur.

Sand    Mudstone    Amber    Tar    Minerals

## TYPES OF FOSSILS

Animals and plants have been preserved in sand, ice, tar, peat, amber (the resin of ancient trees) and mud, which over time turns to stone. Plants often leave fossilized impressions. Insects may be may be trapped in amber. Replacement fossils are created when minerals replace the original body of an organism.

Trilobite cast    Trilobite mould

## MOULDS AND CASTS

Sometimes, a buried fossil is destroyed completely but leaves behind a natural mould in the surrounding rock. The space left in the mould may then be filled with more minerals, creating an accurate cast of the fossil's shape. The cast and the mould fit together perfectly.

## How a fossil is formed

Fossils form in several ways, each of which creates a different type of fossil (see left). One of the most common types occurs when minerals fill pores in the hard tissues of an animal or plant and solidify. The soft parts of the organism rot away, leaving a fossil.

### 1. DECAY

The slowly decaying carcass of a dead *Procolophon* reptile lies exposed on the Earth's surface.

### 2. BURIAL

Shallow streams sweep sediment such as sand and gravel over the reptile's body until it is completely buried.

### 3. FOSSILIZATION

Under pressure over millions of years, sand around the skeleton turns to rock, and the bones become a fossil.

### 4. EXPOSURE

The process of erosion, together with natural movements of the Earth, expose the fossil at ground level.

### PREPARING THE FOSSIL

Scientists carefully excavate and clean fossils. If necessary, they piece several together to show what an animal looked like.

Procolophon fossil

| HADEAN | ARCHAEAN | PROTEROZOIC | | | | | | | |
|--------|----------|-------------|--------|--------|--------|--------|--------|--------|--------|
| PRE-CAMBRIAN TIME | | | PALAEOZOIC | | | | | | |
| | | | CAMBRIAN | ORDOVICIAN | | SILURIAN | DEVONIAN | CARBONIFEROUS | PERMIAN |
| 4,560 | | 545 | 495 | | 443 | 417 | 354 | 290 | 248 |

MILLIONS OF YEARS AGO (MYA)

# Evolution

EVOLUTION IS THE PROCESS by which organisms change
over generations as they adapt to changing environments.
Small ancestors may give rise to larger animals, such
as the elephant, but evolution may also bring about a
reduction in size, or the loss of redundant features,
such as wings or flippers. New species may evolve
from populations that become separated from the rest.

## Natural selection

British scientist Charles Darwin
(1809–1882) noticed that
members of a species vary
from each other slightly, and
that these differences are
passed on to the next
generation. Those born with
the most useful differences
are better at competing for
food, and produce the most
offspring. He called this
natural selection.

Akiapolaau *searches
for insects with
downcurved
upper bill.*

Liwi's *beak and tubular tongue
are suited to sipping nectar.*

Apapane *has
useful multi-
purpose beak.*

*Original species
of honeycreeper.*

Maui parrotbill
*uses lower bill for
chiselling into
wood for insects.*

Kauai akialoa
*has long beak
for winkling
out insects.*

Kona finch *has
strong bill for
crushing seeds.*

## HAWAIIAN HONEYCREEPERS

Today, there are 23 species of small, finch-like birds
called honeycreepers living on the Hawaiian islands.
They are probably descended from a single species
of honeycreeper. Over thousands of years, different
kinds of honeycreepers gradually evolved, each with
a unique beak to feed on a certain type of food.

## EVOLUTION OF ELEPHANTS

Living things do not evolve over a single
lifetime. Instead, they change as one
generation and species follows another.
The earliest elephants were small,
with short tusks and trunks. As time
went by, their tusks,
trunks and
bodies
changed.

Moeritherium

Phiomia

Gomphotherium

Deinotherium

Woolly mammoth

Asian elephant

| PHANEROZOIC | | | | | | | | | AEON |
|---|---|---|---|---|---|---|---|---|---|
| MESOZOIC | | CENOZOIC | | | | | | | ERA |
| SSIC | CRETACEOUS | TERTIARY | | | | | QUATERNARY | | PERIOD |
| | | PALAEOCENE | EOCENE | OLIGOCENE | MIOCENE | PLIOCENE | PLEISTOCENE | HOLOCENE | EPOCH |
| 142 | 65 | 55 | 34 | 24 | 5 | 1.8 | 8,000 BC | PRESENT | |

# Dinosaur tree

THE DINOSAURS FIRST APPEARED about 230 million years ago, and were the world's dominant life forms for more than 165 million years. Thousands of different dinosaur species trod the Earth during the Triassic, Jurassic and Cretaceous periods. Each may have survived no more than two to three million years before becoming extinct. Scientists classify them all according to a family tree that shows how they evolved from the very first dinosaur. All except the birds vanished in a mass extinction at the end of the Cretaceous period.

DINOSAUR ANCESTORS

### Essential dinosaur facts

●Dinosaurs were reptiles, and shared many features with reptiles alive today, including scaly skin, sharp claws, and young that hatch from eggs.

●Dinosaurs were land-dwelling animals, but were closely related to the pterosaurs, or flying reptiles, and to the crocodilians, which were at home in water.

●Scientists place all known dinosaurs into one of two groups, named according to the structure of their hips: bird-hipped dinosaurs (ornithischians) and lizard-hipped dinosaurs (saurischians).

●More than 500 species of dinosaur have been identified so far, but this is probably only a tiny percentage of those that existed.

●Most scientists now believe that birds are a type of feathered dinosaur.

Lesothosaurus

FABROSAURS

EXTINCT

*The fabrosaurs were small, lightly built plant-eaters.*

ORNITHISCHIANS

*During the Triassic, dinosaurs evolved into two types – the ornithischians and the saurischians.*

SAURISCHIANS

HERRERASAURS

Anchisaurus

PROSAUROPODS

Dilophosaurus

*The theropods were a big group of two-legged carnivores.*

THEROPODS

*Coelophysoids, such as Dilophosaurus, were among the earliest theropods.*

Herrerasaurus

EXTINCT

TETANURANS

*Herrerasaurs were small to medium-sized predators of the Triassic.*

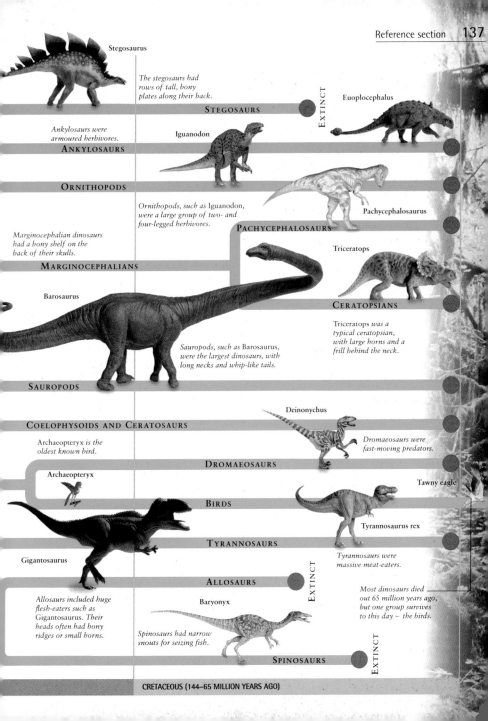

Stegosaurus

*The stegosaurs had rows of tall, bony plates along their back.*

**STEGOSAURS** ●

Euoplocephalus

*Ankylosaurs were armoured herbivores.*

Iguanodon

**ANKYLOSAURS**

**ORNITHOPODS**

Pachycephalosaurus

*Ornithopods, such as Iguanodon, were a large group of two- and four-legged herbivores.*

**PACHYCEPHALOSAURS**

*Marginocephalian dinosaurs had a bony shelf on the back of their skulls.*

Triceratops

**MARGINOCEPHALIANS**

Barosaurus

**CERATOPSIANS**

*Triceratops was a typical ceratopsian, with large horns and a frill behind the neck.*

*Sauropods, such as Barosaurus, were the largest dinosaurs, with long necks and whip-like tails.*

**SAUROPODS**

Deinonychus

**COELOPHYSOIDS AND CERATOSAURS**

*Archaeopteryx is the oldest known bird.*

*Dromaeosaurs were fast-moving predators.*

**DROMAEOSAURS**

Archaeopteryx

Tawny eagle

**BIRDS**

Tyrannosaurus rex

**TYRANNOSAURS**

Gigantosaurus

*Tyrannosaurs were massive meat-eaters.*

**ALLOSAURS** ●

Baryonyx

*Most dinosaurs died out 65 million years ago, but one group survives to this day – the birds.*

*Allosaurs included huge flesh-eaters such as Gigantosaurus. Their heads often had bony ridges or small horns.*

*Spinosaurs had narrow snouts for seizing fish.*

**SPINOSAURS** ●

**CRETACEOUS (144–65 MILLION YEARS AGO)**

### PROTOMAMMALS
(Shrew-like insect-eaters)

*Probably laid eggs.*

Morganucodon

**EXTINCT**

Ptilodus

*Multituberculates had unique teeth with many cusps, or "bumps".*

### MAMMAL
### ANCESTORS

### MULTITUBERCULATES
(Small plant-eaters resembling squirrels, mice or opossums)

### MONOTREMES
(Platypuses and echidnas)

*Young hatch from eggs.*

Alphadon

Argyrolagid

### MARSUPIALS
(Kangaroos, opossums, bandicoots and their relatives)

*Young develop inside pouch on mother's body.*

### XENARTHRANS
(Anteaters, sloths, and armadillos)

### AFROTHERES
(Elephants, hyraxes and sea cows)      Moeritherium

### RODENTS AND RABBITS
(Squirrels, rats, mice, rabbits, and their relatives)

### PRIMATES
(Monkeys, apes, lemurs and lorises)

Plesiadapis

### INSECTIVORES AND BATS
(Shrews, moles, hedgehogs, bats and their relatives)

Bat

### CREODONTS

Miacis

*Embryo nourished inside mother through an organ called the placenta.*

### CARNIVORES
(Cats, dogs and their relatives)

### PLACENTALS

### PERISSODACTYLS
(Horses, rhinos and tapirs)

Basilosaurus

# Mammal tree

**MAMMALS ARE BACKBONED** animals that have hair, suckle their young with the female's milk, and maintain a constant body temperature. They first appeared during the Triassic period. But there were relatively few kinds of mammal until the late Cretaceous and Palaeocene, when many new types emerged, including rodents, elephants, carnivores and primates. This tree shows how mammal groups are related and when they may have appeared.

TRIASSIC (248–206 MYA)   JURASSIC (206–142 MYA)   CRETACEOUS (142–65 MYA)   PALAEOCENE (65–55 MYA)   EOCENE (55–34 M

*Monotremes alive today have long snouts, no teeth and lay eggs.* Platypus

*Marsupials produce tiny, naked offspring that feed on milk in a special pouch.* Kangaroo

Thylacosmilus

*Xenarthrans have special joints in their backbone and relatively few teeth.*

Elephant

Armadillo

*Afrotheres are a varied group that originated in Africa.*

Megatherium

Rabbit

*Rodents and rabbits have constantly growing incisor teeth.*

Rat

Lemur

*Primates have dextrous hands and feet, and flat nails on the fingers and toes.*

Humans

*Insectivores eat invertebrates. Many have well-developed snouts and small eyes and ears.*

Mole

Hyaenodon

Dinofelis

EXTINCT

*Carnivores have pointed front teeth called canines, often used for slicing flesh.*

Dog

*Creodonts had short faces and large canine teeth.*

Hipparion

*Perissodactyls are odd-toed – they walk on one or three toes.*

Rhino

Cow

Daeodon

*Artiodactyls are even-toed – they walk on two or four toes.*

### ARTIODACTYLS

(Antelopes, deer, cattle, sheep, camels, hippos and pigs)

### WHALES

(Whales and dolphins)   *Whales and dolphins are aquatic, almost hairless and have flipper-like limbs.*

Whale

### EXTINCT SOUTH AMERICAN HOOFED MAMMALS

(Mammals resembling camels, horses, hares, etc.)

EXTINCT

Macrauchenia

# Extinction events

**AN EXTINCTION EVENT OCCURS** when many thousands of species die out within a relatively short time. There have been many such events in the Earth's past. Most happened gradually over several million years, and were caused by a series of factors rather than by any single catastrophe. However, at least five events, shown on the graph below, resulted in extinctions on such a scale that most of the Earth's life perished. We may never be sure what caused such mass death, but the main theories are outlined here.

Eruptions fill the Earth with gas and ash, or fill the atmosphere with volcanic dust, which blocks out light and causes plants to die. Eruptions also pump out poisonous gases, which produce acid rain.

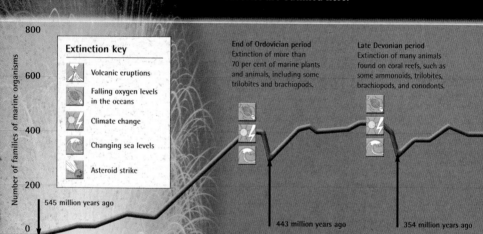

**Number of families of marine organisms**

800

600

400

200

0

### Extinction key

- Volcanic eruptions
- Falling oxygen levels in the oceans
- Climate change
- Changing sea levels
- Asteroid strike

545 million years ago

**End of Ordovician period**
Extinction of more than 70 per cent of marine plants and animals, including some trilobites and brachiopods.

**Late Devonian period**
Extinction of many animals found on coral reefs, such as some ammonoids, trilobites, brachiopods, and conodonts.

443 million years ago

354 million years ago

## The sixth mass extinction?

With the world's population doubling every 40 years, today's environments are being destroyed at an unprecedented rate by human activity, with catastrophic consequences for plant and animal life.

• Intensive farming, grazing and pesticides are reducing soil fertility and destroying ecosystems and wild animal habitats.

• Animal species are becoming extinct at rates of between 100 and 1,000 times faster than they were before humans arrived.

• An estimated 300,000 animal species have become extinct since 1950. Farming, urban expansion, pollution and the spread of non-native species are drastically reducing animal diversity.

• Half of the world's terrestrial species live in forests, which are being cut down at the rate of 1 per cent a year.

• Hi-tech industrial fishing is exhausting fish stocks and leading to the disappearance of previously common fish in many seas.

• Pollution by industrial chemicals and fossil fuels is destroying marine organisms through water contamination and oil spills.

## CLIMATE CHANGE

The Earth's climate does not stay the same, but gradually changes over time. These changes may alter a species' habitat so much that it fails to adapt and dies out. Climate change may come about through volcanic activity, which pours carbon dioxide into the atmosphere, causing a greenhouse effect; shifts in the tectonic plates may carry warm regions to the poles, and vice versa, and changes in the Earth's tilt and orbit may make climates warmer or colder.

Hot dry climates create deserts

Ice caps expand in cold climates

*Fossil brachiopod shells allow scientists to chart the timing of mass extinctions.*

## SEA LEVELS

Sea levels have always risen or fallen as the climate changes. During warm phases, ice at the poles melts, and sea levels rise. During cold periods, water is locked up as ice on mountains and at the poles, and sea levels fall. Rising seas drown species living on low islands, but inshore sea creatures are left high and dry when seawater drains away. In addition, lack of oxygen in the sea due to slow circulation may cause many marine species to suffocate.

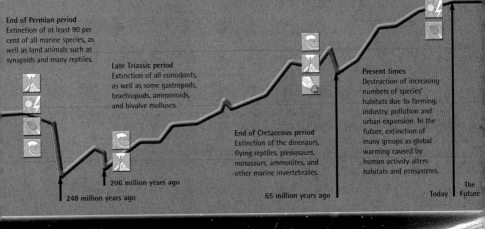

**End of Permian period**
Extinction of at least 90 per cent of all marine species, as well as land animals such as synapsids and many reptiles.

**Late Triassic period**
Extinction of all conodonts, as well as some gastropods, brachiopods, ammonoids, and bivalve molluscs.

**End of Cretaceous period**
Extinction of the dinosaurs, flying reptiles, plesiosaurs, mosasaurs, ammonites, and other marine invertebrates.

**Present times**
Destruction of increasing numbers of species' habitats due to farming, industry, pollution and urban expansion. In the future, extinction of many groups as global warming caused by human activity alters habitats and ecosystems.

248 million years ago

206 million years ago

65 million years ago

Today | The Future

## CATASTROPHIC COLLISION

A large asteroid smashing into the Earth would explode with the force of tens of thousands of nuclear bombs, causing firestorms and tsunamis to race around the world. Dust from the impact would block out the Sun's light for years, making the climate intensely cold and dark. Most plants and animals would die.

# Glossary

Words in *italics* have their own entry in the glossary.

## A

**Aeon** The longest unit of geological time. The four aeons are the Hadean, Archaean, Proterozoic and Phanerozoic.

**Algae** Primitive plants and plant-like organisms that grow in wet conditions.

**Ammonites** An extinct group of coiled-shelled *cephalopods*.

**Amniotes** *Tetrapod vertebrates* whose young develop inside a protective membrane called the amnion. Amniotes include *reptiles*, *birds*, and *mammals*.

**Amphibians** Cold-blooded *tetrapod vertebrates* whose young use gills to breathe.

**Anapsids** A group of primitive *reptiles* with no skull opening behind the eye. Living anapsids include turtles and tortoises.

**Anthropoids** The higher *primates*: monkeys, apes and humans.

**Archosaurs** ("ruling lizards") A major group of *reptiles* that originated in the Triassic. It includes *dinosaurs*, *pterosaurs*, and *crocodilians*.

**Arthropods** Jointed-legged *invertebrates* with a hard outer skeleton. Living examples include insects and spiders.

**Artiodactyls** Hoofed *mammals* with an even number of toes. Includes pigs, camels and deer.

**Asteroids** Rocks of various sizes moving in space throughout the Solar System.

**Australopithecines** ("southern apes") Extinct ape-like *hominids*. Ancestors of humans.

## B

**Big Bang** Violent explosion that gave birth to the *Universe* about 14 billion years ago.

**Bipedal** Walking on hindlimbs rather than on all fours.

**Birds** In evolutionary terms, *dinosaurs* whose forelimbs have become wings and whose scales have become feathers.

**Black smokers** Chimney-like vents in the ocean floor emitting volcanically heated water.

**Bovoids** ("ox-like") *Artiodactyl* hoofed *mammals* including pigs, hippopotamuses and camels.

**Brachiopods** Marine *invertebrates* with a two-hinged shell that protects the soft body.

**Burgess Shale** The site in British Columbia, Canada, where Middle Cambrian *fossils* have been discovered.

## C

**Carnivores** Any meat-eaters, especially the Carnivora – a group of *mammals* including cats, dogs and bears.

**Cephalopods** Marine *molluscs* with large eyes and tentacles. Examples include *ammonites* and squid.

**Ceratopsians** ("horned faces") *Bipedal* and quadrupedal, plant-eating, *ornithischian dinosaurs* with a deep beak and bony frill at the back of the skull.

**Ceratosaurs** ("horned lizards") One of the two major groups of *theropod dinosaurs*.

**Chordates** Animals that have a *notochord*, a rod that gave rise to the backbone.

**Class** Name given to a group of organisms containing one or more related orders.

**Continental drift** The movement of continents across the surface of the Earth over time.

**Core** The very hot, metallic centre of the Earth, which probably has a liquid outer layer and a solid interior.

**Creodonts** An extinct group of carnivorous *mammals* that thrived in the Palaeocene *epoch*.

**Crust** The solid outer layer of the Earth.

**Crustaceans** A large class of *arthropods* named after the shell that encases their bodies. Includes crabs and shrimp.

**Cyanobacteria** Blue-green *algae* that make food with the help of the energy in sunlight.

**Cycads** Palm-like, seed-bearing plants that are topped by a crown of fern-like leaves.

**Cynodonts** ("dog teeth") Extinct, dog-like *synapsids* that included the ancestors of *mammals*.

## D

**Diapsids** A group of reptiles with two holes in the skull behind each eye. Diapsids include lizards, crocodiles, *dinosaurs*, and *birds*.

**Dinosaurs** ("terrible lizards") A great group of advanced *archosaurs* with erect limbs.

**Diversify** To become more varied. In *evolution*, when a few *species* evolve into many *species*, which are adapted to survive in different environments.

**DNA** Deoxyribonucleic acid, the molecules of which carry genetic information from one generation to the next.

## E

**Elasmosaur** ("metal plate lizard") A long-necked type of plesiosaur: marine *reptile* with paddle-like limbs.

**Embryo** An animal or plant in its early stage of development from a fertilized egg or seed.

**Epoch** An interval of geological time that is longer than an age and shorter than a *period*.

**Era** A unit of geological time that ranks below an *aeon*.

**Eukaryotes** ("having a true nucleus") All organisms made of cells with a nucleus. Eukaryotes evolved from *prokaryotes*.

**Evolution** The process by which inherited changes produce new *species* from old.

**Extinction** The dying-out of a *species*, caused by competition for resources or unfavourable changes in the environment.

**Extinction event** A series of natural factors which together result in a mass *extinction*.

## F

**Filter feeder** A creature that feeds by filtering plankton and other tiny marine organisms.

**Food chain** A chain of organisms, each dependent on the next as a source of food.

**Fossil** The remains of a prehistoric organism preserved naturally over time.

## G

**Gastropods** The largest *class* of *molluscs*. Their internal organs are carried in a spiral shell.

**Genus** A group of related organisms ranked between the levels of family and *species*.

**Gondwana** The vast southern *supercontinent* that existed between *Pre-Cambrian* times and the Jurassic *period*.

**Graptolites** ("writing on the rocks") Extinct, tiny marine animals that lived in colonies.

**Greenhouse effect** The process by which certain gases in the atmosphere trap heat and warm the Earth's climate.

## H

**Habitat** The natural home of an organism.

**Hadrosaurs** ("bulky lizards") The duck-billed *dinosaurs*. *Bipedal* or quadrupedal Cretaceous *ornithopods* that used their beaks for browsing.

**Herbivore** Any animal that eats only plants.

**Hominids** The group to which humans and their extinct ancestors belong.

**Hominoids** The group of *anthropoid primates* to which humans and apes belong.

**Homo** The *genus* including today's humans and their extinct closest relatives.

# I

**Ice ages** *Periods* of time when much of the Earth's surface is covered by ice sheets.

**Ichthyosaurs** ("fish lizards") Mesozoic marine *reptiles* that resembled modern dolphins.

**Invertebrates** Animals without backbones.

# J K L

**Lobe-finned fishes** A group of fishes with fleshy lobes that supported their fins.

# M

**Mammals** Warm-blooded, hairy *vertebrates* that suckle their young with milk.

**Marsupials** *Mammals* whose young mature in a skin pouch on the mother's belly.

**Mantle** The layer of the Earth's interior between the *crust* and the *core*.

**Megalosaurs** ("great lizards") A mixed group of large carnivorous *dinosaurs*.

**Mesonychians** Extinct, carnivorous, hoofed *mammals* of the Tertiary *period*.

**Meteorite** A fragment of rock that has fallen from space.

**Mid-ocean ridge** A long submarine boundary where two plates are spreading apart.

**Missing link** A supposed undiscovered creature that links our ancestors to the apes.

**Molluscs** A great group of *invertebrates* including bivalves, gastropods, and *cephalopods*.

**Mosasaurs** Large, Cretaceous marine *reptiles* – long-jawed aquatic lizards with slender bodies and flipper-like limbs.

**Multituberculates** Small, rodent-like *mammals* of Late Jurassic to Early Cenozoic times.

# N

**Natural selection** In *evolution*, the natural "weeding out" of weaker individuals and *species*.

**Nautiloids** A type of *cephalopod* living in a straight or coiled chambered shell.

**Neanderthal** An extinct *species* of *hominid* that is closely related to our own species.

**Notochord** An internal rod that stiffens the body of *chordates*. It forms the basis of the backbone in *vertebrate* animals.

# O

**Omnivore** An animal that eats many types of food.

**Ornithischians** ("bird hips") One of the two major *dinosaur* groups (see also *Saurischians*). All were two-legged or four-legged *herbivores*.

**Outgassing** The release of carbon dioxide, steam and other gases from *volcanoes*.

# P

**Palaeontology** The scientific study of *fossil* organisms.

**Pangaea** The *supercontinent* formed at the end of the Palaeozoic *era*.

**Parareptiles** Primitive *reptiles* including all the reptiles known as *anapsids*.

**Period** The unit of geological time between *era* and *epoch*. Periods are an era's main subdivisions.

**Perissodactyls** The "odd-toed" hoofed *mammals*, including horses and rhinoceroses.

**Permafrost** Permanently frozen ground.

**Placentals** *Mammals* whose unborn young are nourished through a placenta.

**Placoderms** ("plated skins") A class of jawed fishes, protected by armour-like plates.

**Plesiosaurs** Long-necked Mesozoic marine *reptiles* with flipper-shaped limbs.

**Pre-Cambrian** The vast span of time from the Earth's formation to the Cambrian *period*.

**Predator** Any animal or plant that preys on animals for food.

**Primates** The group of *mammals* that includes lemurs, monkeys, apes, humans, and their ancestors.

**Proboscideans** Elephants and their extinct ancestors and relatives – mostly large *mammals* with a long trunk.

**Prokaryotes** Tiny, primitive organisms without a cell nucleus. They comprise the bacteria and archaebacteria.

**Prosauropods** Early plant-eating *saurischian* dinosaurs of the Late Triassic and Early Jurassic.

**Pterosaurs** ("winged lizards") Skin-winged, Mesozoic flying *reptiles* – *archosaurs* related to the *dinosaurs*.

# Q R

**Ray-finned fishes** Fishes with fins supported by a ray of bony rods. Includes most fishes alive today.

**Reptiles** Lizards, snakes, turtles, crocodiles and *dinosaurs*. Living reptiles are cold-blooded, scaly *vertebrates* that lay eggs or give birth on land.

# S

**Saurischians** ("lizard hips") One of the two major *dinosaur* groups (see also *Ornithischians*). Most were meat-eaters but many were *herbivores*.

**Sauropods** ("lizard feet") Huge, plant-eating, quadrupedal *saurischian* dinosaurs, including the largest-ever land animals.

**Species** In the classification of living things, the level below a *genus*.

**Stegosaurs** ("plated lizards") *Herbivorous* dinosaurs with two rows of bony plates and/or spines running down the back.

**Stromatolites** Fossilized, mushroom-shaped colonies of *cyanobacteria* that grew from the seabed.

**Supercontinent** A prehistoric landmass containing two or more major continental plates.

**Synapsids** A group of *tetrapod* *vertebrates* that includes the extinct pelycosaurs and

*therapsids*, and the therapsids' descendants, the *mammals*.

# T

**Tectonic plates** The moving segments of the Earth's *crust* that float upon the *mantle*.

**Teleosts** A great group of the *ray-finned* bony fish. Most living fish are teleosts.

**Terror birds** Large, carnivorous, flightless *birds* of the Tertiary *period*.

**Tetanurans** ("stiff tails") One of the two major groups of *theropod* dinosaurs.

**Tetrapods** ("four feet") Four-legged *vertebrates*.

**Therapsids** ("beast arches") Prehistoric *synapsids* that included *cynodonts*, the ancestors of *mammals*.

**Theropods** ("beast feet") The predatory *dinosaurs*, armed with sharp teeth and claws.

**Trilobites** ("three lobed") Extinct marine *arthropods* with external skeletons divided lengthwise into three lobes.

**Tsunami** A huge wave generated by a submarine earthquake, *meteorite* strike or landslide.

**Tyrannosaurids** ("tyrant lizards") A family of huge, *bipedal*, carnivorous *dinosaurs* with large heads and short arms.

# U

**Universe** The entirety of everything in existence.

# V W X Y Z

**Vascular plant** Plants with supporting fibres and inner tubes that act as channels for moisture.

**Vendian** The last *period* of the *Pre-Cambrian*, when complex, many-celled creatures appeared in the sea.

**Vertebrates** Animals with a backbone made up of vertebrae.

**Volcano** A vent or fissure in the Earth's *crust* that releases lava from the *mantle*.

# Index

## Acknowledgements

Dorling Kindersley would like to thank:
Chris Bernstein for the index; Sheila Collins
for design assistance; Ben Hoare and Alyson
Lacewing for editorial assistance; Mark
Longworth and Jurgen Ziewe for their
digital illustrations and Bedrock Studios
for their digital dinosaur models.

The publisher would like to thank the
following for their kind permission to
reproduce their photographs:
(Abbreviations key: t=top, b=bottom,
r=right, l=left, c=centre)

alamy.com: 58, 65tc, 84-85; American
Museum of Natural History: (image
5860(2)40cl, 120bl, 128bl;Bruce Coleman
Ltd: Natural Selection 16-17, Pacific Stock
16tl, Jen & Des Bartlett 80cl; S. Conway
Morris/Cambridge University: 21cra;
Corbis: Tom Bean 24cr, Buddy Mays 36cl,
17br, Rick Price 24tr, Galen Rowell 51c,
Tomas Sanchez 54bc, Steve Wilkings 57tl,
Nigel Dennis/Gallo Images 59crb, David
Muench 60-61bc, Charles Mauzy 62-63,

Kevin Schafer 64tl, 65bc, Scott T Smith 72-
73, Paul A Souders 74tc, 76bc, Bill Stormont
89bc, Jason Burke/Eye Ubiquitous 91clb,
92-93, Galen Rowell 92tl,O. Alamany & E.
Vicens 95r, Kevin Schafer 96-97, Anthony
Bannister 110crb, 102, 104-105, 112br
(bkgrd), Tom Bean 113br, Paul Edmondson
116-117, 118-119, Rose Hartman 128c,
Gallo Images 123cra; J M Cameron 133cra,
Roger Ressmeyer 140cla, Peter Johnson
141tc; German State  Museum of Nature
63cra; Oxford University Museum 47cra;
Pitt Rivers Museum 127cra, 127cr, 130cla;
Royal British Columbia Museum 124bl;
Royal Museum of Scotland 22tl; Royal
Tyrell Museum Canada 75tr; Geoff Dore:
3cbl, 6cl; GeoScience Features Picture
Library: 27clb; Seapics.com: Doug Perrine
58cb, 60tc; FLPA - Images of nature: Panda
Photos 7cb, 16-17, Martin Withers 92-93;
Masterfile UK: 3c; David Noton 90; Dr
Mark A.Purnell, University of Leicester:
28cl; Nature Picture Library Ltd: David
Shale 24c; The Natural History Museum,
London: 15br, 17cr, 48bl, 57br, 82cfb, 106tc,
109cr, 116bl, 118cl, 122tl, 131tr; N.H.P.A.:
Pete Atkinson 2bcr, B Jones & M Shimlock

26crb, 29br, Daniel Heuclin 52-53, Laurie
Campbell 34-35, Nigel Dennis 108c, Pete
Atkinson 36bc; Oxford Scientific Films:
Ashod Francis/AA 32-33,Daniel Cox 124-
125, DPL/OSF 114-115, E R Degginger
113tr, E R Degginger/AA 129tr; Royalty
Free Images: Photodisc Blue/Getty 60-61tc,
62tl; Science Photo Library: Mauro
Fermariello 1, 2,Matthew Bate 2bl, Tony
Craddock 2bcl,Vaughan Fleming 2br, Keith
Kent 2bc, BSIP/CHAIX Bernhard Edmaier
3br, Sinclair Stammers 3cbr, Matthew Bate
4tl, Mehau Kulyk 4, BSIP/CHAIX 5cla,
ESA 5b, Bernhard Edmaier 5clb, Dr Leon Golub
6bl, 7ca, Simon Fraser 7clb; Mark Garlick
8bl; Louise K Broman 9cra, 9bc; Bernhard
Edmaier 10-11, Michael Dunning 11tr,
11cra, Manfred Kage 12cl, Simon Fraser
14c, Sinclair Stammers 14cb, Dr Leon Golub
& John Reader 15tc, Tony Craddock 18, Dr
Leon Golub 18bl, Dr Steve Gull & Dr John
Fielden 19ca, Keith Kent 26, Dr Leon Golub
26, 36bl, Dr Steve Gull & Dr John Fielden
37ca, Peter Scoones 41br,Vaughan Fleming
44, Dr Leon Golub 44bl, Dr Morley Read
46bl, John Eastcott & Yva Momatiuk 46-47,
Louise K Broman 51crb, Martin Land 53cr,

Dr Juerg Allan 56tl, Steve Gull & Dr Jo
Fielden 59ca, Dr Leon Gubb 66bl, Drs S
Gull & John Fielden 67ca, D Van
Ravenswaay 76cb, Dr Leon Golub 76bl,
Dr Steve Gull & Dr John Fielden 77ca,
Bernhard Edmaier 78tl, Martin Dohron
Stephen Winkworth 84tc, Prof. Walter
Alvarez 88cla, D Van Ravenswaay 88cr
NASA 88bl, Dr Steve Gull & Dr John
Fielden 91cal, Pekka Parvianen 100cla;
Planetary Visions Ltd 103cla, Gusto 10
John Heseltine 106-107, Alfred Pasieka
109cb, Planetary Visions Ltd 111ca, Joh
Reader, 114cb, Tom van Sant, Geosphe
Project/Planetary Visions 121tr(bkgrd)
Bernhard Edmaier 122, Volker
Steger/Nordstar - 4 Million years of M
123cb, 132bc; Novosti 132tc, BSIP 139c
John Foster 140-141, B C E Alexander
141ca, Louise K Broman 141tr, Julian F
142-143, 144; Stephen Alvarez; Pete Atkin
39tr, Jeff Hunter 40-41, Brett Baunton
71tr, Gary Buss 94, Andrew Mounter 5
Brett Baunton 136, Roine Magnusson
101; University of Michigan: 56br; Warr
Photographic: Jane Burton/Warren
Photographic 67c, 74tl.